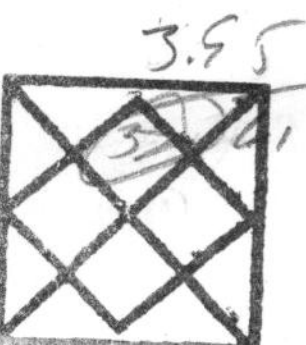

Michel Anguier's Pluto: The Marble of 1669

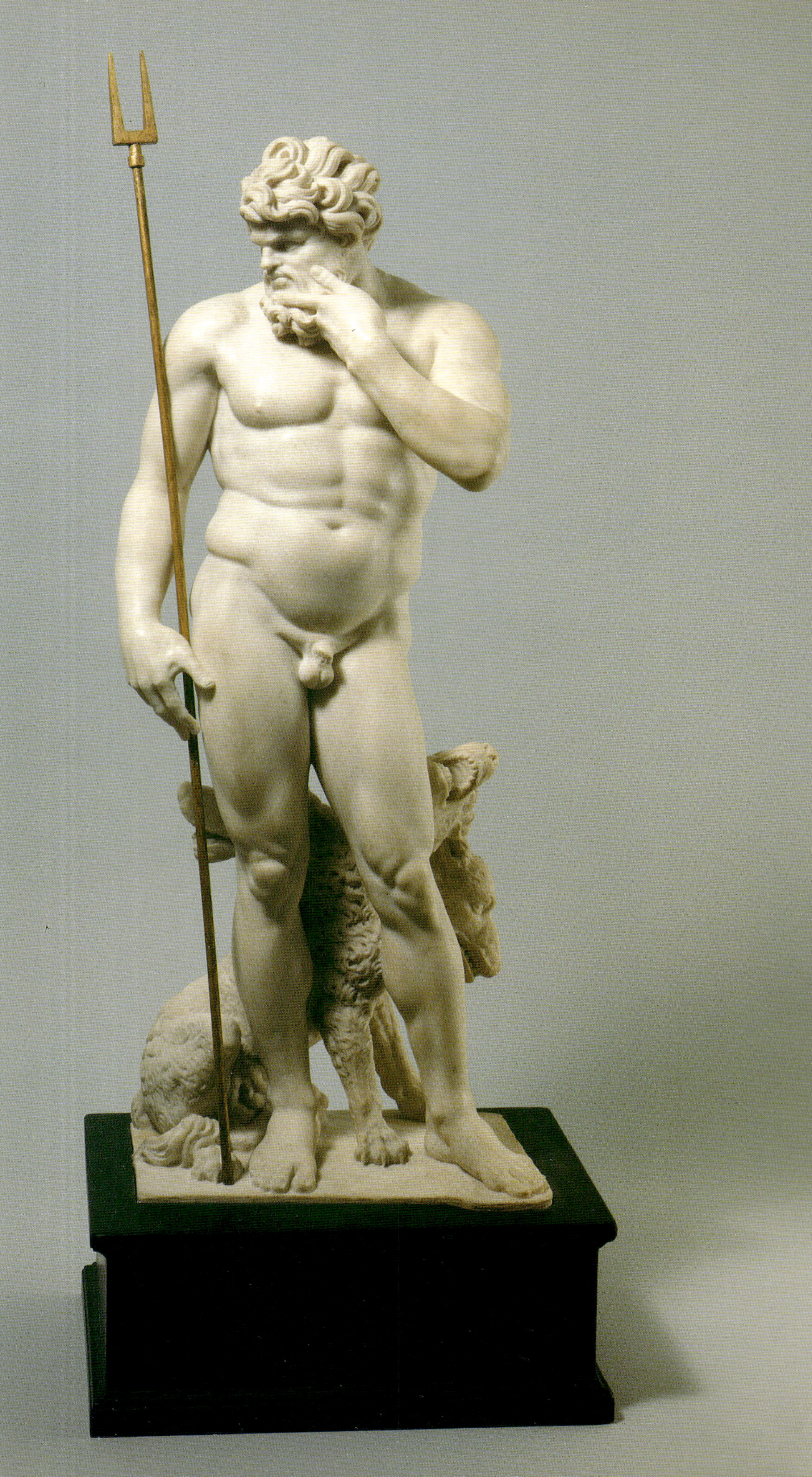

Michel Anguier's Pluto: The Marble of 1669

NEW LIGHT ON THE FRENCH SCULPTOR'S CAREER

Bernard Black
and
Hugues-W. Nadeau

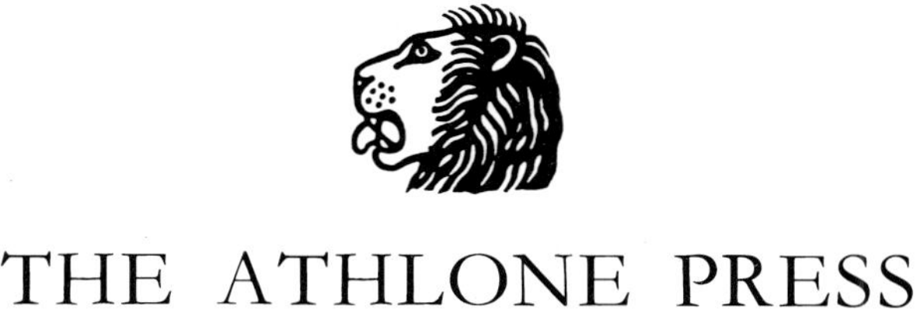

THE ATHLONE PRESS

London & Atlantic Highlands, NJ

First published 1990 by The Athlone Press Ltd
1 Park Drive, London NW11 7SG and
171 First Avenue, Atlantic Highlands, NJ 07716

British Library Cataloguing in Publication Data
Black, Bernard
Michel Anguier's Pluto: the marble of 1669: new light on the French sculptor's career.
1. French sculptures. Anguier, Michel
I. Title II. Nadeau, Hugues-W.
730.92
ISBN 0-485-11400-3

Library of Congress Cataloging in Publication Data
Black, Bernard
Michel Anguier's Pluto: the marble of 1669: new light on the French sculptor's career / by Bernard Black and Hugues-W. Nadeau.
p. cm.
Includes bibliographical references (p.) and index.
ISBN 0-485-11400-3 (cloth)
1. Anguier, Michel, 1612 or 14–1686. Pluto. 2. Anguier, Michel, 1612 or 14–1686—Criticism and interpretation. 3. Pluto (Greek deity)—Art. 4. Classicism in art—France. I. Nadeau, Hugues-W., II. Title.
NB553.A54A69 1990
730'.92—dc20

Jacket and frontispiece illustration:
A colour version of PLATE 1

Produced for the publishers by
John Taylor Book Ventures,
Hatfield, Herts

Designed by Malcolm Preskett
Made and printed in Great Britain by
BAS Printers Limited, Over Wallop,
Stockbridge, Hants

Contents

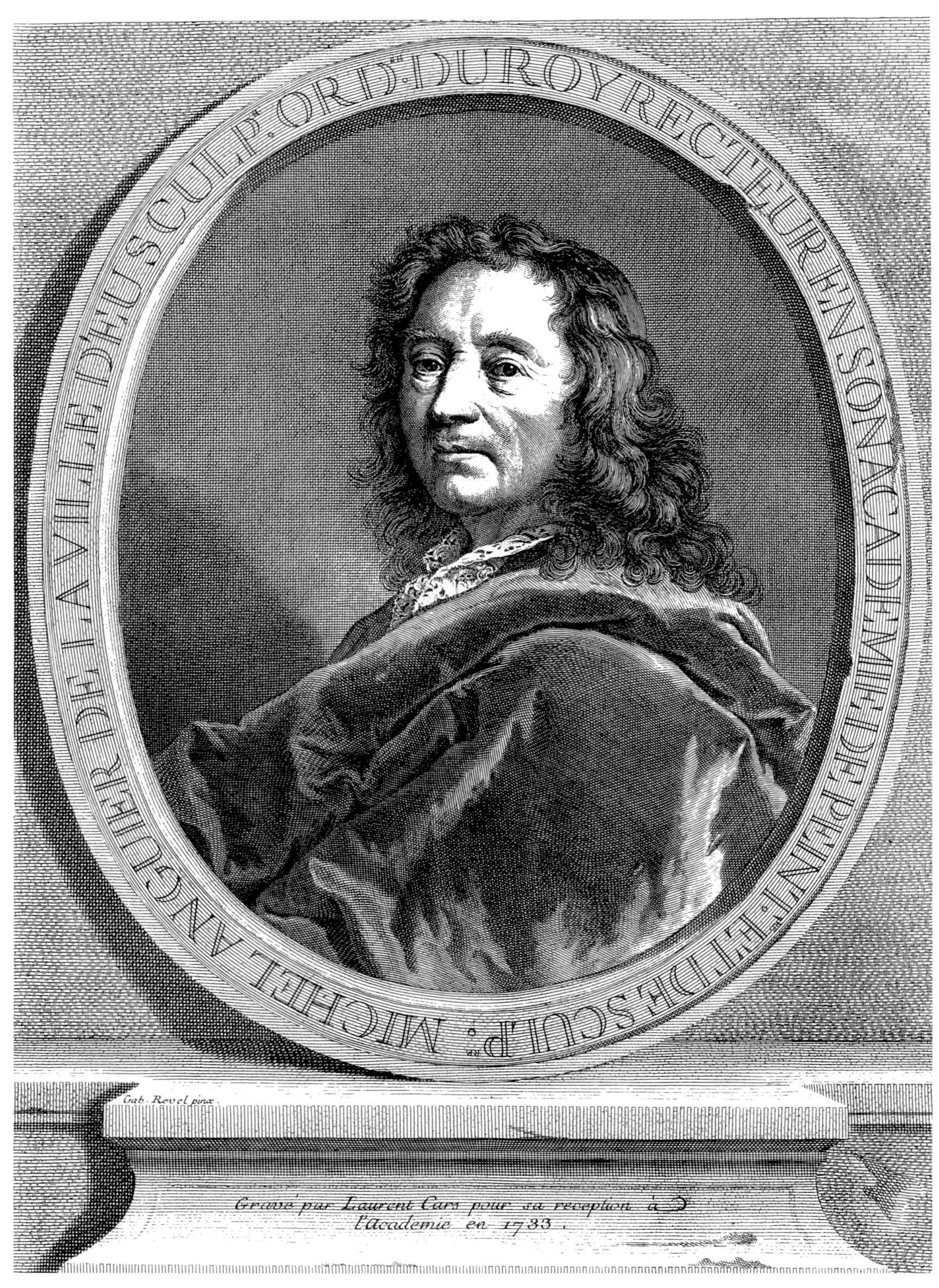

Laurent Cars, Portrait of Michel Anguier (1612–1686), engraving, dated 1733, after the painting by Gabriel Revel which was his *morceau de réception* to the *Académie*, in 1683.
Wolfenbüttel, Herzog August Bibliothek, Portr. II, 81.

Preface and Acknowledgements

At its inception, it had been decided that our study would be limited to the documentation and the stylistic evaluation of an exceptional small marble group of *Pluto and Cerberus*, after the model by Michel Anguier (1612–1686). In so doing, however, we gradually became involved with various aspects of the life, work and teaching of this remarkable seventeenth-century French master, an inventive sculptor of whom little is generally known. A reconsideration of a contemporary report on his 1669 lecture to the Royal Academy of Painting and Sculpture, in which the sculptor displayed the figure of a *Pluto* 'by his hand' to demonstrate his theories, supported the discovery of evidence, at first art-historical and ultimately scientific, that it was Michel Anguier who carved the present statuette.

Obviously, we are fully aware that we have touched narrowly upon a broad subject; however, our research has led us into the writing of this extended study which contains important and previously unpublished documentation on Michel Anguier, thus contributing, we believe, to a greater knowledge of the sculptor and to a better understanding, not only of the artist himself, but also of his influence on the sculptors of the period of Louis XIV and the School of Versailles.

We would like at this point to express our gratitude to Olga Raggio for her interest in our work from an early stage and, later, for her encouragement to publish our findings. Special thanks must also go to Anthony Radcliffe for his judicious remarks and for his opinion which finally convinced us to proceed with the publication.

We are indebted to Professor François Souchal whose observations on an initial study were most helpful, and to Geneviève Bresc-Bautier who, after discussing a first draft, pointed out the difficulties ahead and emphasised the importance of finding *the* proof, which only reinforced our determination. We are also grateful to Professor Thomas Hedin for his considered review of a preliminary paper, prior to our discovery of significant new documentation, and for his thought-provoking comments.

Introduction: Biographical Background

The period covered by this monograph on Michel Anguier's marble *Pluto* is the third quarter of the seventeenth century in France and runs from the invention of the model in 1652 to the sculptor's retirement in 1678.

These years include the eventful 1660s, the decade after the death of the aged Jacques Sarrazin (1588–1660), when Anguier had already become an established master. The death of Cardinal Mazarin in 1661 had prompted the start of the *règne personnel* of Louis XIV; this was followed by the arrest and imprisonment of the *Surintendant* Fouquet, by the prodigious rise of Colbert and by the ascendance of Le Brun. In 1662, Queen Anne d'Autriche, the King's mother, who had been *Régente* during his minority, gave Michel Anguier his most important commission for the extensive sculptural decoration of the stone interior of the Church of the Val-de-Grâce. It consisted of a complex programme in which the surfaces of vaults, all the arcades and the spandrels beneath the dome, were carved with reliefs by Michel himself; he executed, as well, the marble group of *The Nativity* for its high altar, which is his great masterpiece. It was a monumental project, given to the best sculptor of the time in Paris, which was to occupy him almost entirely for five years. It was also at the end of this decade that Michel's lectures at the *Académie* began (1669) and that the marble *Pluto* would have been carved.

Although a detailed knowledge of Anguier's career is not essential to the study of the marble *Pluto*, a brief review of it will contribute to an appreciation of this master. Similarly, an *aperçu* of the earlier period of his life will indicate the background of and the influences on the sculptor. Michel was born in Normandy, the son of a carpenter. He went to Paris in 1627, aged 15, to join his brother François Anguier (1604–1669), at first as an apprentice and afterwards as an assistant in the atelier of Simon Guillain (1581–1658), recognised as an accomplished sculptor with a vigorous style. Little is apparently known of Michel's early years and there is no accredited personal *oeuvre* until he left for Rome in 1641. There, he joined Alessandro Algardi's workshop where his status has been described recently by Jennifer Montagu as that of 'another of Algardi's pupils', suggesting that he was a young and untried '*giovane*' (apprentice). This must be erroneous: as we have seen, Michel was almost thirty when he arrived in Rome with up to fourteen years' experience behind him, with Guillain in Paris. It is, surely, more likely that he was employed by Algardi as a trained assistant, with some seniority, and this would explain why, for example, in the three reliefs for the Lateran which he modelled after that master's designs, there was no slavish following of Algardi's style but a quite personal interpretation. Michel remained in Rome for ten years and, although his Roman works display a distinctly Baroque manner, it is probably true to say that the impression made upon him by that city's antique sculpture was more profound and enduring than that of the prevailing style. This classical influence is evident in the sculpture he was to execute on his return to France. That only a comparatively small body of work has been ascribed to Michel during his many years assisting Algardi is intriguing: he must have been involved in other, apparently undocumented, projects to support himself and he probably enjoyed a certain freedom to spend time studying the antique and making plaster copies to take home.

Back in Paris in 1651, Michel assisted his brother François, an outstanding sculptor whose *oeuvre* consisted mostly of funerary monuments and who was then working on the tomb of the Duc de Montmorency. However, the paths of the two brothers soon diverged as Michel's personal reputation rapidly became established and he was given several commissions of his own including, as early as 1651, the model for a statue of Louis XIII, which was cast in bronze larger than life-size for the city of Narbonne. By 1653, his renown had earned him a prestigious commission from the *Régente*, Queen Anne d'Autriche, for the elaborate stucco sculpture to decorate her apartments in the Palace of the Louvre. This was followed, from 1655 to 1658, by his employment by the *Surintendant* Nicolas Fouquet (which, at that time, was second only in importance to working for the *Régente*) for all the sculpture at his elegant residence of Saint-Mandé, followed by numerous sculptures for his château and park of Vaux-le-Vicomte. In the years which followed, Michel continued to be in demand and his production was such that, as Louis Gonse has noted, it becomes difficult to follow; even his deep commitment to the Val-de-Grâce did not exclude other commissions.

In contrast to Michel's extraordinary years when his time had been fully occupied, the period following 1670 saw a distinct decline in his activities as a sculptor. In 1672 he was briefly involved in the creation of a catafalque for Chancellor Séguier which was a tribute to their late patron and first *Protecteur* by the entire *Académie*, of which Anguier was by then a rector. Unlike so many sculptors of the period, he was not favoured with any involvement at Versailles' seemingly endless construction due, not to his age, but, as will be discussed later in this study, to the antipathy between him and Le Brun. However, the seventies offered Michel an activity which he found equally rewarding: his carefully-prepared lectures, or *conférences*, at the *Académie* which gave him the opportunity to expound on his theories on art and anatomy. They were to influence a new generation of sculptors.

In 1674, as if to crown his career, he started working on the reliefs and sculptures for the Porte Saint-Denis, a triumphal arch commissioned by the city of Paris to commemorate the military victories of Louis XIV, which demonstrated a perfect harmony between architecture and sculpture and was one of Michel's great achievements. In 1678, he announced his formal retirement and in the same year Jean Pesne, the engraver, dedicated to Michel Anguier his suite of engravings of *The Labours of Hercules*, after the drawings by Poussin, as a tribute to the master. Michel, however, completed at least one more commission, an impressive marble *Christ crucified, alive*, well over two metres in height, for the main altar of the Sorbonne. Michel Anguier died in 1686 and was buried in his parish church of Saint-Roch in Paris, next to his brother François. It cannot be coincidental that it was to this same church that two of his few marble carvings were relocated after having been confiscated from their original installations during the Revolution: in 1803, the *Christ* from the Sorbonne was installed in Saint-Roch's Chapelle du Calvaire and, two years later, his much-admired *Nativity* from the Val-de-Grâce was placed on the altar of its oval Chapelle de la Vierge, under the dome.

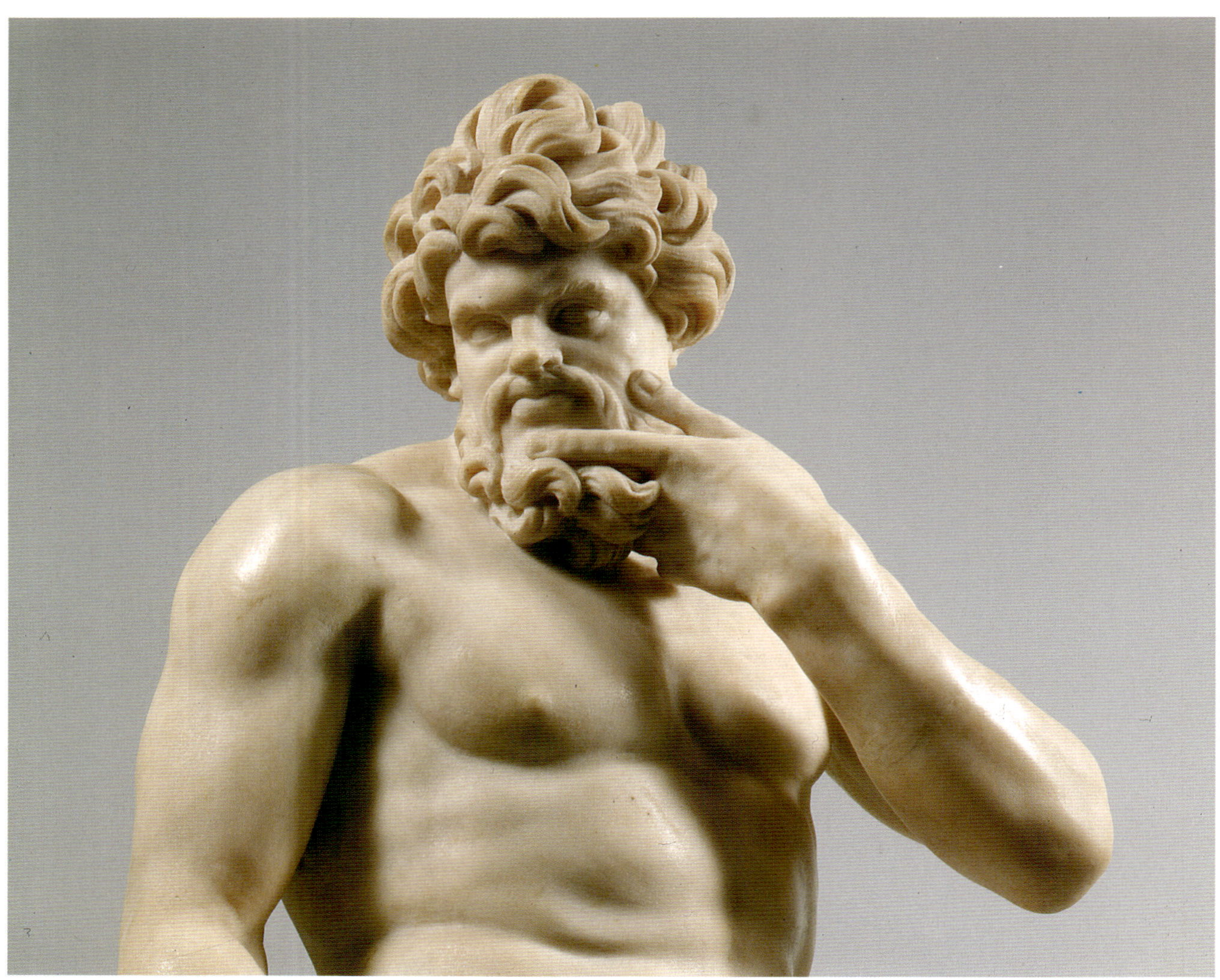

'. . . Several have tried to persuade me that his head is too small for his large body but it is his great muscles . . . which tend to make it look smaller . . .'
– Michel Anguier on the Hercules Farnese, in his lecture to the *Académie* in 1669.

I

The Marble Pluto Discovered

MONTE CARLO, 1983. In the December auction sale of the estate of Monsieur Hubert de Saint-Senoch, lot 210 in the catalogue was a small, finely-carved marble statuette of a muscular standing figure with a snarling, three-headed dog behind him. Across the front of the marble base, a bold, carved inscription read 'LE GROS FECIT'. M. de Saint-Senoch had lived for many years in the Pavillon de Bidaine, an attractive old mansion in the Provençal countryside near Aix, which he had furnished in an appropriate manner for such a residence – good French furniture and decorations, Old Master and nineteenth-century paintings, Oriental porcelains and also a few pleasing sculptures. Lot 210, which had stood in the entrance-hall of the Pavillon, balanced by an eighteenth-century Dutch marble statuette of *Amphitrite* of similar proportions, was described in the catalogue as a '*Statue d'Hercule par Le Gros*', a fair description, given the visual evidence. However, to anyone familiar with French bronzes of the seventeenth and eighteenth centuries, the sculpture was puzzling: the model was a familiar one, long known to be *Pluto*, not *Hercules*, and derived from a series of small figures of mythological gods and goddesses, first modelled in 1652, which were the point of departure for several French seventeenth-century marble or stone garden statues and a number of bronze versions, executed well into the eighteenth century, if not later. The original, mid-seventeenth-century models were by the French sculptor, Michel Anguier, and the succeeding carved or cast versions were usually attributed in the literature or in catalogue entries as also being by him. Thus, the Saint-Senoch marble appeared to have been carved after Michel Anguier by one of the two important French sculptors named Le Gros, Pierre I (1629–1714) or his son, Pierre II (1666–1719), although neither of these was known to have had any professional association with Anguier.

As will be demonstrated, however, the sculpture is unquestionably seventeenth century and, more importantly, is a previously unpublished carving by Michel Anguier himself. The 'signature' was added many years after the original execution by someone ignorant of the author of the invention, a circumstance not uncommon in the eighteenth and nineteenth centuries.[1]

To begin with a description of the sculpture, it is a white marble figure of the god Pluto, the ruler of the underworld, accompanied by his attribute, the three-headed watchdog Cerberus. This statuette, originally carved from one block of marble, shows Pluto naked, standing with his head turned to the right, his left hand raised to his face, the thumb and forefinger resting pensively against his beard, the right hand spread against the thigh, supporting a two-pronged fork. At his feet and behind him, the dog, which has heads of three different breeds, snarls angrily. The total height of the marble sculpture is 73 cm and the height of the figure alone is 68.5 cm (Plates 1–4). With its present wood base, the height is 82 cm.

Given the scale of this marble, unusually small for the period in France, and its composition, which was, as Charageat noted, an invention both personal and original,[2] the problems of carving have been resolved in a masterly demonstration of the sculptor's skill, apparent as much in the deep undercutting of the locks of hair as in the subtle observation of the anatomy. However, beyond the technical achievement, this figure of *Pluto*, which conveys his moody temperament as well as the heaviness of his muscled body, exemplifies the essential principles of Michel Anguier's life-long preoccupation with the relationship between anatomy and emotion and its representation in sculpture.

Comparison with other carved marbles by the sculptor is made difficult by the fact that no such work still extant is to be found in any museum or private collection.[3] Thus the rarity of this marble statuette, while enhancing its importance, complicates the task of documenting it as a work by Michel Anguier.

Concerning its condition, one may say that, overall, *Pluto* is in an excellent state of conservation except for the right hand, which is a recent reconstruction after the original invention.[4] The dog, Cerberus, is in equally good condition but the muzzle of one head is an old replacement, possibly from the sculptor's workshop. The edges of the base have been reduced, after sustaining damage, with the signature 'le gros fecit' added at that time, probably after 1750 (Plate 39).[5]

Documented information on the sculpture's history is sparse; the fact that it was not in Anguier's *atelier* shortly before he died[6] implies that it was disposed of in his lifetime. Nor was it in the *inventaire après décès* of his nephew and heir, the sculptor David Bourderelle (1706).[7] Exhaustive research, as yet not completed, does not rule out, however, the possibility that, towards the end of his life, Michel gave it to someone outside his family to whom he felt indebted.[8] Coming to the eighteenth century, it is probably the figure of *Hercules and Cerberus*, which was in the collection of Monsieur de Villemandi until March 1788, when it was included in a Paris sale of his estate as *'Hercule enchaînant Cerbère, signée du nom de Legros'* (Plate 38).[9] Following this catalogue entry, it is listed by Souchal as 'presumably' by Pierre II Legros.[10] Research has not, so far, uncovered the identity of eighteenth-century owners prior to M. de Villemandi, although the possibility that it belonged to a Mme de Julienne in Paris, before 1778, cannot be excluded.[11] In this century, we know that it was in the collection of M. de Saint-Senoch until it was included in the sale of his estate by Sotheby Parke Bernet Monaco on 4 December 1983.[12] It now is in the collection of the authors.

NOTES TO CHAPTER I – numbers 1 to 12

1. To cite one notable example of this wide-spread ignorance of authorship: Jacques Saly's marble *Faun holding a goat* (1751), which was his *morceau de réception* to the *Académie*, is in the Getty Museum. It bears a spurious signature, giving the carving to N. F. Coustou in 1715. (Ref.: *The J. P. Getty Museum Journal*, vol. 14, 1986, p. 257, no. 229.)

2. Charageat, 1968, p. 116.

3. The large marble figure of *Amphitrite* in the Louvre, commonly described as 'by Michel Anguier', was carved between 1680 and 1684 by the *praticien* Nicolas Massé, as Charageat has documented (1968, p. 122). The only marble carvings which can be given securely to the sculptor's own hand are his masterpiece, *The Nativity*, now in the Church of Saint-Roch in Paris and the large *Christ crucified, alive*, formerly in the Sorbonne, now also in Saint-Roch. Examples of his carvings in stone are similarly few: the extraordinary programme executed for the interior of the Church of the Val-de-Grâce, the reliefs on the Porte Saint-Denis, both in Paris, and the two large figures of goddesses from Saint-Mandé now in the Metropolitan Museum (*Leda*) and the Toledo Museum of Art (*Amphitrite*).

4. The sensitive reconstruction of this hand in marble is by Anne Brodrick of the Sculpture Conservation Department of the Victoria and Albert Museum. She is also responsible for the entire conservation, as well as the re-creation of the god's two-pronged fork, following the original design.

5. Old restorations to this statuette were made on two occasions. Chronologically, the first of these was after damage to the muzzle of Cerberus' right-hand head. The front section of this muzzle had been broken off and restored or replaced. The close similarity of the marble used, its working and surface wear suggest that the accident happened at the time of, or shortly after, the original execution.

   The second, and more serious, accident was to the right hand and may be theorised as follows: a study of the underside of the marble base of *Pluto* reveals that it was conceived to be set into a socle or plinth which would explain why the surface under the base is *convex*, making it impossible for the group to stand upright by itself (see Plates 42 and 43). At some time, probably in the second half of the eighteenth century, the figure was forcibly levered out of its socle, resulting in what was, presumably, irreparable damage to Pluto's right hand, originally open and resting against his thigh. A new hand, now discarded, was then carved, conceived to hang, fist closed, in a gesture which could be interpreted as a grasp (Plate 39). There were also two clean breaks to the left arm and, finally, the damage to the base itself brought about by the pressure exerted from the leverage. The underside was left roughly-hewn but there is still a small flat area remaining on it, set at an angle (Plate 43), and, projecting this to all four sides, a sketch can be made proposing how the original shape might have appeared

(PLATE 44). Also, the base was trimmed in an uneven shape, the spurious signature added and the sides raked with a tool.

6. Germain Brice, *Description de la ville de Paris*, 2nd ed., 1687, vol. I, pp. 68–69. This information was first conveyed to us by Prof. Thomas Hedin.

7. Publ. M. Rambaud, *Documents du Minutier central concernant l'histoire de l'art: 1700–1750*, vol. II, pp. 413–414 and 1028–1030. Again, we are grateful to Prof. Hedin for this further information.

8. Slow progress in this research is due to the fact that several archival documents which should normally be readily available are oddly missing, or misfiled.

9. Although the word '*enchaînant*' suggests an action not apparent in this composition, the use of the word can be attributed to the whim of the cataloguer of the Villemandi sale, based on the then clenched fist of the god. This supposition seems more likely than that there were in existence two similar marble figures of Pluto/ Hercules and Cerberus, both '*signée du nom de Le Gros*', particularly as seventeenth-century marbles such as the present one are rare. One may ask why the inscription on the marble attributed this carving to 'Legros' (Pierre I Legros or Pierre II Legros) and not to Michel Anguier. This presupposes that not only was the identity of the sculptor unknown but also that the marble was originally unsigned. Following the creation and the embellishment of the park at Versailles in the seventeenth century, which continued into the early eighteenth century, the name of Pierre I Legros as one of the principal sculptors involved in the carving of classically-inspired figures must have come easily to mind for such a figure as *Pluto*. The reputation of Pierre II Legros, on the other hand, was made in Rome where he worked almost exclusively (except for one brief return to Paris) and it is unlikely to have been in his name that the signature was chiselled. It should also be pointed out that the style of the present marble carving is quite different from that of Legros II or, for that matter, of Legros I.

10. Souchal, 1981, vol. II, p. 299, no. 54.

11. Françoise de la Moureyre, collaborator with Prof. Souchal on *French Sculptors*, 1977–87, has drawn our attention to a marble statuette in the estate sale of Madame de Julienne (Paris, 5 Nov. 1778, lot 109) described in the catalogue as '*Pluton, de 25 pouces de proportion* (67.5 cm) *sur son socle de 6 pouces d'élévation* (16.2 cm). *Cette statue paraît avoir été faite à Rome par Legros.*' Given that the height of the Julienne marble appears to correspond to that of the present *Pluto* (68.5 cm), if both measurements are taken from the upper surface (*terrasse*) of the base, one cannot exclude the hypothesis that it was purchased by M. de Villemandi, who would therefore have been responsible for adding the 'signature'. If this were the case, this 1778 catalogue entry would be an indication of the original height of the base of the marble *Pluto* being studied. However, the lack of any mention of Cerberus (as in the Villemandi entry), even for an eighteenth-century description, somewhat weakens the

possibility that the Julienne *Pluto* is the same sculpture.

12. When it was in the Saint-Senoch collection, the marble figure was set in a shallow, unfinished wood base which enabled it to stand (the inside having been gouged to take the curvature of the marble), with the inscription 'LE GROS FECIT' visible in front (PLATE 39). As the signature is apocryphal, a new slate-coloured wood base was provided and the sculpture was lowered into it, concealing the later inscription (PLATE 45). This base can easily be removed for inspection by resting the figure on its back and unfastening the two screws holding the marble (PLATE 43).

II

The Published Knowledge of Michel Anguier's 'Melancholy' Pluto

To this date, Michel Anguier's invention of a *Pluto* figure has been known to us through the bronze versions of the model (which are discussed in Appendix B), through two engravings, neither of which was executed earlier than the beginning of the eighteenth century and, finally, through the published literature on his *oeuvre*.

Every biographer of Anguier, beginning with Guillet de Saint-Georges in 1690,[13] has noted that in 1652, shortly after his return to Paris from Rome, the sculptor modelled a series of six figures of gods and goddesses,[14] each 18 *pouces* (48.6 cm),[15] which were cast in bronze for Monsieur Laurent de Montarsis, *joaillier du Roi*, and which included a '*Pluton mélancolique*'.[16] This series of figures was studied more particularly by Marguerite Charageat in 1968 and Ian Wardropper in 1976. While the latter's article is largely restricted to the bronze versions, Charageat concerned herself also with the larger than life-size carvings in *pierre de tonnerre*, after the same models, which were commissioned from Anguier in 1655 by Nicolas Fouquet for his château at Saint-Mandé. She also included in her list of known representations of the *Pluto* figure two engravings, one after drawings by René Charpentier (1680–1723) for the series of plates known as the *Galerie de Girardon*, and the other by Louis Desplaces (1682–1739)[17] for a series of plates that the Chalcographie of the Louvre lists in its catalogues as illustrating sculptures 'in the gardens of Versailles'.[18]

Charpentier's drawing of the *Pluto* in Girardon's collection of sculpture was published about 1710 but was the result of a project which had commenced in 1706.[19] The illustrated *Pluto*, wearing a fig-leaf and holding a two-pronged fork, is described (no. 40 in the legend on the plate) as a '*modèle de terre cuite par M. Anguier*' (PLATE 8).

No size is given but, after a comparative examination of the other drawn sculptures on this plate, this *modèle* may be demonstrated to be of a similar height to several which are listed in Girardon's *inventaire après décès* as being '*environ deux pieds et demi*', that is 'approximately' 80 cm and similar in scale to the present marble. That Michel modelled on this scale is confirmed by two terracotta figures of gods (*Mars* and *Minerva*) documented in the *inventaire après décès* of his nephew, David Bourderelle, also as being '*deux pieds et demi*'.[20]

It should be emphasised here that the word '*modèle*' is used, rather than '*figure*' as in the description of other terracotta sculptures also illustrated on the same plate. By definition, a model is preparatory to a final work, usually in a different material. As Girardon was involved personally in the preparation of these engravings of his *Galerie* and was an admirer (and one-time collaborator) of Michel Anguier, one must accept that these descriptions are correct and that he was aware that, in this instance at least, Michel's terracotta *Pluto* was intended to be (or had been) executed in another medium, possibly marble.[21]

However, besides the bronze versions, the principal source for the knowledge of the invention and of its author in much of the recent literature has been the early eighteenth-century engraving of *Pluto*, draped and without a fork, by Louis Desplaces (PLATE 10). The source for Desplaces' *Pluto* is important for it was roughly contemporary (after 1710) with the *Galerie de Girardon* engravings and yet it is unlikely that Desplaces followed these or was even familiar with Girardon's terracotta *modèle* by Anguier. The two engravings follow the same invention but show significant variations (compare PLATES 9 and 10).[22]

That Desplace's engraving could not have been after a Versailles marble, as the literature often asserts, will be demonstrated in Appendix A on Michel Anguier's limited involvement in the sculpture programmes for the park. The existence of a large stone version carved by Michel for Fouquet, referred to above, is documented and Charageat apparently saw it in Paris in 1968 in what she called a 'completely ruined' condition. After Fouquet's arrest in 1661, his possessions were dispersed at a sale in 1665 when the stone figure of *Pluto* was purchased by the Marquis de Louvois whose widow removed it in 1696 to her château of Choisy, known later as Choisy-le-Roy,[23] (along with seven other stone deities by Anguier) where it remained through the eighteenth century. There is therefore the possibility that Desplaces saw the large stone *Pluto* at Choisy. Alternatively, he might have followed one of the more detailed bronzes. It should be noted here that Desplaces did not always depend on direct observation for his compositions but is known to have used other artists' drawn or painted versions for his sources.[24] Yet, notwithstanding, his fanciful engraving of the god, often with a later, erroneous legend placing the figure in the park at Versailles, has been cited widely in the literature, until recently, as documentation that a large marble *Pluto* by Michel Anguier existed at one time.

NOTES TO CHAPTER II – numbers 13 to 24

13. Dussieux, *Mémoires*, vol. I, pp. 436–450.

14. These were, as listed by Guillet de Saint-Georges (op. cit., p. 438), '*un Jupiter foudroyant, une Junon jalouse, un Neptune agité, une Amphitrite tranquille, un Pluton mélancolique, un Mars qui a quitté ses armes et une Cérès éplorée*'.

15. A *pouce* is equivalent to 2.7 cm. Under the *Ancien Régime* the unit of measure for length was the *pied*, corresponding to 32.4 cm, divided in twelve equal parts, each called a *pouce*. (*Dictionnaire Le Petit Robert.*)

16. The material of the original six models (stucco or terracotta) was never specified and they have probably been destroyed. Neither have the bronzes cast for Monsieur de Montarsis, which would have been the cited 48.6 cm high, survived or been identified to this day.

17. Charageat, 1968, p. 119.

18. For an early catalogue entry containing this assertion, see *Chalcographie au Musée Impérial du Louvre*, 1860 edition. Desplaces' engraving of *Pluto* is listed under no. 1393. References to Desplaces' engravings in the literature on Anguier are frequently erroneous because they are usually based on these old *Chalcographie* catalogues. From another source came the extravagant claim that they dated from 1679, which is three years before Desplaces was born. (Ref. *Barockplastik am Niederrhein*, Kunstmuseum Düsseldorf, 1971, entry no. 319, p. 352.) His original engravings never specified the location of the illustrated gods by Michel as Versailles; this was added in later editions.

19. These engravings, after drawings by Girardon's pupil René Charpentier, have been related by Souchal to the inventory of François' collections of sculptures drawn up after his death (see bibliography). However, the *modèle* of *Pluto* illustrated in the *Galerie de Girardon* is not in the inventory, which suggests that it was disposed of earlier by Girardon.

20. The engraved illustrations of the *Galerie de Girardon* are informative concerning size because of the inclusion of the terracotta *Pluto* cited. It is known that the collection, for the purpose of presentation, was arranged in imaginary settings and that sculptures were grouped to create a well-balanced effect. From observation, one realises that the size of certain figures has been adapted by the artist to fit this scheme, but it seems unlikely that they were all totally thrown out of proportion and bore no relation to one another. Indication of this comes from the inventory after Girardon's death, published by Souchal, which, although generally vague, lists nonetheless a number of entries with the approximate sizes. On the plate which includes the *modèle* of *Pluto*, a figure stands directly above (inv. no. 261) described as '*une figure de terre cuite d'un Apollon d'environ 2 pieds*' (which is 64.8 cm). The *Pluto* is drawn slightly larger, which suggests between 70 and 80 cm, the same

proportions as the present marble. At the extreme right and left of the shelf where *Pluto* stands are '*2 figures de terre cuite*' representing Girardon's allegories of the months of October and November (inv. no. 265, also '*environ 2 pieds de haut*'). The proportions of these four terracottas appear to conform with those of the various antique busts illustrated on the same plate which (if entry no. 279 for '*cinq bustes de marbre environ deux pieds et demy*' is indicative) were 'about' 81 cm, a normal height for a marble bust.

While no definite conclusion on scale can be drawn from these comparisons, they are quite indicative, particularly in conjunction with the two Michel Anguier terracotta gods of '*deux pieds et demi*' that were owned by his nephew. These are cited and documented by Bresc-Bautier (p. 9, no. 3) and were apparently models for two large marble statues, commissioned for the Tuileries, which were initially executed to the final size in stucco but never carved in marble (Dussieux, p. 442 and note 1).

21. No bronze cast of this terracotta *modèle* in Girardon's *Galerie* (which would have been between 70 and 80 cm high) is known. The Montarsis casts were 18 *pouces* (48.6 cm) and other documented casts of the seventeenth century (e.g. Dresden) are about 24 cm high (9 *pouces*).

22. On the Girardon plate, Pluto is depicted carrying a two-pronged fork but this attribute is missing in Desplaces' engraving. In his *Neptune* engraving, Desplaces gave the god a trident (PLATE 11), which is also seen in most of the bronzes of that model, and it seems logical that he would have depicted Pluto with a fork if the example had been before him: this would have confirmed the identity of his *Pluto* and enhanced it. Furthermore, the position of Cerberus' tail in each engraving is quite different; also, in Desplaces the god is draped and in Charpentier he wears a fig-leaf (compare PLATES 9 and 10).

23. The Marquis de Louvois (1641–1691) became *Surintendant des bâtiments du Roi* upon Colbert's death in 1683, until his disgrace in 1689. Choisy, originally called 'Soisy', belonged by inheritance to the Dauphin (1682–1712) who exchanged it with Madame de Louvois in 1692 for Meudon plus 400 thousand *livres*. Choisy was afterwards sold by the Duc de Villeroy (son-in-law of Madame de Louvois and governor of Louis XV) to the Princesse de Conti whose heir, the Duc de la Vallière, sold it to Louis XV in 1739, thus becoming *propriété du Roi*. From then on, it was referred to as Choisy-le-Roy. (Piganiol de la Force, *Description de Paris*, Paris 1765, vol. 9, p. 137.)

24. '*Ofters stach D. nach Gemälden u. Plastiken nicht unmittelbar sondern erst nach Zeichnungen die er selber oder ein anderer Zeichner (z.b. Nic. Bertin u. Bern. Picart) angefertigt hatten.*' Thieme Becker, vol. IX, p. 144.

III

A Figure of Pluto in Anguier's Lectures of 1669 and 1676: Art, Anatomy and Emotions

As has been observed, Michel Anguier was the best sculptor in Paris when he was given the prestigious commission for the Val-de-Grâce.[25] By 1667, when the five-year project had been completed, he was 55 years old and an established master, widely respected by his contemporaries. It may therefore seem surprising that he had still not joined the *Académie royale de Peinture et de Sculpture* to which most of the talented artists of the time belonged. The explanation is simple: he, along with Pierre Mignard, had been in open feud with Charles Le Brun, the director of the *Académie*, and both had refused to submit to his discipline by joining that eminent institution.[26] The act would have been interpreted, in effect, as their acceptance of Le Brun's domination and the awarding of any commissions deriving from the *Académie* would have meant working after Le Brun's designs, thus subordinating themselves to his autocratic rule. To repress their own proven talent for invention in this way would certainly have been anathema to both men. One may ask, then, why Anguier did change his mind and join the *Académie* in 1668. If his protector, Colbert,[27] may have been influential in this decision, undoubtedly the principal reason for this turnabout was to take part in the round of *conférences* which had been reintroduced in 1667.[28] Anguier must have attached great importance to the opportunity to expound on his theories and it may be assumed that there was a tacit understanding that the move did not involve any participation in the sculpture programmes of Versailles.[29]

For his first *conférence* of the ninth of November, 1669, Michel chose to discuss the subject of the *Farnese Hercules* and to relate it to his theories on art and anatomy. Until H. van Helsdingen published the original full text of this *conférence* in 1983, only a summary of it, written by someone present in the room at the time, had been published by Henri Stein in 1889. In this summary, it is reported that Michel spoke of a figure of *Pluto* which was 'by his hand' and which earned the admiration of everyone who saw it.[30] What was this figure of *Pluto* and what special qualities could it have had to provoke such extravagant praise? Although it is not mentioned by Guillet de Saint-Georges in his *Mémoire* on the works of Michel Anguier, read to the *Académie* in 1690, the existence of this figure of *Pluto* by Michel is irrefutable, documented as it is by the reference to it in the records of the *Académie*.[31]

A reading of Michel's own original manuscript of this *conférence* is enlightening.[32] In it, proceeding to describe at some length the anatomy and the character of Pluto, the sculptor says (writers' italics): 'As we see by *this* figure of *Pluto* that I have represented in a cold and arid melancholy . . .'[33] and further, on the anatomy of Pluto as opposed to that of Hercules: '. . . the melancholic temperament of *this one here* is completely opposite to that of our great Hercules . . .'[34] and, again, when speaking of Hercules and the interaction of his 'muscles and the quality of his flesh that is firm and vigorous and not soft like the flesh and muscles of *this one here* . . .'.[35] The implication is obvious that a figure of *Pluto*, executed by Michel, was standing next to him and was being used for demonstration. It also seems clear that the very detailed references to the *Pluto* imply that it was a finished work which demonstrated the characteristics that Michel wished to emphasise.

There followed, from 1669, a series of lectures at the *Académie* by Michel Anguier in which he elaborated his preoccupation with anatomy, the movement of muscles and their relationship to a hierarchy of emotions and temperaments. Thus, on the first of August, 1676, he gave his *conférence* on '*De la manière de représenter les Divinités selon leur tempérament*' in which he described ten gods and goddesses, including Pluto, of whom he said: 'This God Pluto *here* should be of short and strong proportions, the expression on his face indicating melancholy . . . his flesh heavy and moist . . . his muscles plump and sagging . . .'[36] Once again, the words used in referring to this god are evidence that Anguier was pointing to a figure of *Pluto* actually in the room: when he says 'here' he uses the old French spelling of the word '*icy*', meaning 'right here'. In fact, Pluto is the only one of the *Divinités* to which the word '*icy*' is applied.

Again, what was this *Pluto* of 1676? It must be assumed, logically, that it was the same sculpture shown at his *conférence* of 1669; it is unlikely that there were two. For practical reasons, it could not have been the large stone carving from Saint-Mandé, even if it had been available, and would have had to have been small enough to be moved easily.

Given the documented reaction to his *Pluto*, cited above, to assume that it was a small bronze statuette like the one which belonged to Laurent de Montarsis is unreasonable. The Comte de Caylus in his *Mémoire* read to the *Académie* on the third of May, 1749, referred to the series of statuettes owned by the jeweller as 'nothing marvellous', having apparently seen them.[37]

Although Michel was a master in the art of working in stucco, again it seems difficult to accept that a plaster or stucco figure could be refined sufficiently to meet the exacting description of the *Pluto* he demonstrated in the two *conférences*.

It could have been a terracotta but it seems doubtful that it was the terracotta *modèle* which was later owned by Girardon and which was, we know, a preliminary work intended for translation into a different medium. Even acknowledging the possibility that this *modèle* was displaying all the subtlety and the characteristics that Michel emphasised in his *conférences*, it should be remembered that terracotta was not considered a noble material. By this criterion, a modelled clay, even though highly accomplished, would not arouse the same admiration and command the same respect as a finely carved marble of the same invention. As a demonstration of this, one can cite the masterly terracotta of *Hercules and Atlas* that Michel presented to the *Académie*[38] and which is now in the Louvre[39] (Plate 19). Although this major group is mentioned and described by nearly everyone who has written on Anguier, sometimes associating it with his theories on art and anatomy, the absence of recorded contemporary laudatory comments or later praise supports this argument.[40] The *Pluto* executed by Michel Anguier, to which he was pointing in his *conférence* of 1669, it must be recalled, did evoke a general admiration in the room, vivid enough to be recorded for posterity.

In summary, if the *Pluto* which Michel displayed at the two *conférences* was not the large stone figure from Saint-Mandé, nor a bronze cast or a plaster version, and if it is extremely doubtful that it was a terracotta statuette, then we are left with only one other possibility: that it was a marble carving.

NOTES TO CHAPTER III – numbers 25 to 40

25. Bazin, p. 103: (The interior of the Val-de-Grâce) '*fut confié au meilleur sculpteur du temps . . .*'.

26. Walker, p. 78 (Anguier versus Le Brun); p. 96 (Anguier resisting the rise to power of Le Brun in the 1660s); also Paris, Hôtel de la Monnaie, 1983, pp. 355–356: 'Mignard was (1666) in open rivalry with Le Brun and refused to join the *Académie*'.

27. Dussieux, 1854, vol. I, p. 445 (Guillet de Saint-Georges); p. 461 (Caylus). Also Stein, p. 22.

28. This sound theory has been advanced by Professor Hedin (written communication, 6 April 1986).

29. It is true that a marble of Michel's *Amphitrite* was carved by a *praticien* to decorate the Bosquet des Dômes in Versailles, circa 1680–1684, but this statue, which was a version of the model of 1652, was an exception which does not contradict this assumption. (Ref. Charageat, 1968, pp. 122–123.)

30. Stein, p. 51: '*Là-dessus il parla d'une figure de Pluton qui est de sa main et qui a mérité l'estime de tous les honnêtes gens.*' (For the original manuscript of the complete summary of this *conférence*, refer to Bengy-Puyvallée and note 32 herewith.) To understand the exact meaning of the word '*honnête*' in this statement is essential. This was well explained by Theodore Rousseau Jr. in his introduction to *The Splendid Century: French Art 1600–1715* (Metropolitan Museum of Art, New York 1960, p. 5): 'The ideal of the time was not the superman or hero but rather what was called the "honnête homme" which may be translated as the man of integrity and common sense . . .'. That Michel Anguier's *Pluto* was admired by all such men was indeed a high compliment.

31. Dussieux, pp. 436–450. Guillet's biography is not without errors (Dussieux, p. 445, note 2; p. 446, note 2) and the reason for his not listing the *Pluto* could be, simply, that he had not examined all the records and that he listed only works well in the public knowledge. Also, it was over twenty years since the *conférence* and the sculpture had undoubtedly passed into a private collection long before.

32. The manuscripts from the old *Académie royale de Peinture et de Sculpture*, now in the archives of the Ecole des Beaux-Arts in Paris, have been consulted. There are three manuscripts on Michel's *conférence* of 9 November 1669 (Bengy-Puyvallée, folio no. 136). The first two are in the sculptor's own handwriting and the first of these (34 pages) was published by van Helsdingen in 1983 (with a Dutch adaptation alongside the original version); the second one (24 pages: shorter because it doesn't list all the anatomical measurements) is the one that was read to the *Académie* and it bears at the end of the text, in the hand of Henri Testelin (1616–1695), *sécrétaire* of the *Académie* from 1651 to 1681, the following inscription: '*Prononcé à l'assemblée de l'Académie le neuf novembre 1669 par Monsieur Anguier*'. (Signed) '*H. Testelin*'. The

third manuscript (10 pages) is the one cited by Henri Stein, p. 51. An anonymous note preceding this manuscript ascribes it to Guillet de Saint-Georges but it is not in his handwriting and, in any case, Guillet is later. Neither is it written by Henri Testelin. It was most likely a report by Félibien (André Félibien, 1619–1695), the respected *historiographe des bâtiments du Roi*, who had been appointed by Colbert in 1667 specifically to record each of the lectures at the *Académie* with an '*extrait sommaire par escrit qui contiendrait la substance de ces conférences*', so relieving Testelin from this time-consuming activity. (Montaiglon, *Procès-verbaux*, vol. I, pp. 315–317; and Dussieux, vol. I, p. IX.)

33. van Helsdingen, p. 97: '*Comme nous voions par cestre figure de pluton que nous avons représenté dune melancolie froide et seiche . . .*'.

34. op. cit., also p. 97: '*Lhumeur melancolique de cestui ci est tout contraire a celle de notre grand hercule . . .*'.

35. op. cit., p. 98: '*les muscles et la forme de la chair ferme et reslevée* (of Hercules) *et non abaissée comme la chair et les muscles de cestui ci . . .*'.

36. Stein, p. 63: '*Ce Dieu Pluton icy doit estre d'une basse et forte proportion, l'air de son visage sera mélancolique . . . sa chair pesante et humide . . . les muscles charnus et tombans bas . . .*'.

37. Dussieux, vol. I, p. 455.

38. When Michel Anguier was invited to join the *Académie* in 1668, he had not been required to submit a *morceau de réception* which would, necessarily, have been a marble carving. However, he chose to offer, as a gift, this terracotta *Hercules and Atlas* to the *Académie* when he was admitted to that institution.

39. It is worth noting here that the original, naturalistic terracotta base of this large group suffered damage over the years. At some time, to give it additional support, it was mounted on an octagonal wood base, covered with tinted gesso to simulate terracotta. At least one bronze version of the group is known (Fine Art Museums of San Francisco) which incorporates this octagonal base in the cast.

40. Among those who refer to the terracotta group are: Guillet de Saint-Georges, who only mentions the group (Dussieux, p. 445); Stein (pp. 22–23), who quotes the dry description of it by N. Guérin (*Description de l'Académie*, Paris 1715, pp. 149–150) and adds '*le sujet est traité à l'antique d'après un dessin évidemment rapporté de Rome*'; and Marguerite Charageat (*Louvre catalogue*, 1957, p. 182), who relates it to the sculptor's preoccupation with anatomy. Louis Gonse (p. 170) simply dismisses it.

IV

The Earliest Illustration of Anguier's Pluto: An Unpublished Seventeenth-century Engraving

THE *Réserve* of the Cabinet des Estampes in Paris contains two states of an engraving of Michel Anguier's *Pluto*, given to Gérard Audran but actually by Jean Pesne, which are listed in the two catalogues of the Cabinet's holdings but which have never been otherwise published, certainly not in the literature on Anguier's suite of gods and goddesses. The two engravings are almost identical except for one major variation: the god is naked in the first state (PLATE 12) and wears a fig-leaf in the second (PLATE 13). It was not unusual for two states of an engraved figure to be published and it seems logical that the first, nude, state of *Pluto* represented the god exactly as the sculptor created him. The two states also bear different, later inscriptions which convey conflicting attributions to their authorship.

Robert-Dumesnil catalogued both of these engravings and gave them to Gérard Audran (1640–1703) on the basis of a later inscription in the margin of the 'fig-leaf' state: '*Statue de marbre d'un Pluton et de son chien Cerbère de dix Pieds de haut posée dans le Jardin de Versailles, faite par M. Anguiere. G. audran sculp.*'.[41] This inscription is, however, not in Audran's handwriting and is erroneous,[42] as will be seen in the discussion of Michel's involvement in Versailles. This mistaken 'Gérard Audran' catalogue entry of Robert-Dumesnil was perpetuated in this century by Roger-Armand Weigert when he listed the two *Pluto* engravings in his *Inventaire*.[43] An explanation for the later addition of this inscription could be the fact that Gérard Audran had an active boutique in Paris where he sold works by other engravers, including Pesne, as well as his own. It is documented that he sometimes 'edited' these artists' engravings with his added embellishments.[44] Also, at his death, engravings in his stock without inscriptions were often attributed to him by his successors, without foundation.[45]

The first, or 'nude' state, is more important in the documentation of the marble group of *Pluto* because the god is completely naked, has similarly shaped genitals and also lacks pubic hair, as in the marble. The engravings by Desplaces and Charpentier, the only two such illustrations recorded until now, both depict Michel's *Pluto*, wearing the conventional fig-leaf, or with a drapery. This 'nude' state in the Cabinet des Estampes belonged to Pierre Mariette (1634–1716), known as Pierre II Mariette, an important *marchand d'estampes* and noted collector and grandfather of the famous Pierre-Jean Mariette (1694–1774). As was Pierre II's practice, he added in ink his signature and the date, presumably of its acquisition, 1692, giving us a *terminus ad quem* for the engraving which is a mere six years after Michel Anguier died.[46] It will be demonstrated however that its execution probably dates from the late 1670s. It is therefore the earliest illustration of the *Pluto* or, in fact, of any of the suite of gods and goddesses which Anguier created in 1652.

This 'nude' state is signed in the margin in an old hand: '*pesne scupsit*' and, although this is not in the hand of Jean Pesne, the attribution is undoubtedly correct. A cursory comparison with the engravings of Gérard Audran, such as his treatment of Girardon's *Enlèvement de Proserpine* for example (PLATE 18), gives evidence that the engraving of Michel Anguier's *Pluto* is not in his style. However, a similar comparison with engravings by Jean Pesne, particularly his series of the *Travaux d'Hercule* and several anatomical studies, all after Poussin, demonstrates convincing stylistic affinities (PLATES 16 and 17). Equally significantly, the *Hercule* suite was published in 1678, the year that Michel Anguier announced his retirement[47] and the frontispiece to the published suite of engravings testified handsomely that Pesne conceived, dedicated and presented the suite to the sculptor (PLATE 15). This dedication reads, in translation, as follows: 'THE LABOURS OF HERCULES from the original by N. Poussin the most renowned royal painter, here engraved on copper. Presented as a gift to the truly great Michel Anguier, sculptor to the most Christian King, most deserving Rector of the royal Academy of sculpture and painting, this tribute in everlasting recognition. Conceived and dedicated by J. Pesne'.[48] Jean Pesne's admiration for the master is implicit and he would have been aware of the sculptor's *conférences*, including those of 1669 and 1676 in which Michel discussed Hercules and Pluto and the manner of depicting these gods.[49] That Anguier was pleased by the gesture is indicated by the fact that, in 1679, he presented a bound set of Pesne's *Hercules* engravings to the *Académie* which still exists in the *Réserve* of the library of the Ecole des Beaux-Arts in Paris.[50]

Pesne was considered one of the 'best and most faithful' engravers of Poussin[51] and it is not surprising that he chose Poussin's drawings of Hercules to honour Michel Anguier. To the question of how Pesne had access to Poussin's suite of drawings, one must go back for an answer to their origin as studies for the planned decoration in 1641 of the Grande Galerie du Louvre[52] and to Jean-Baptiste Colbert who, as *Surin-*

tendant des bâtiments du Roi, was in a position to make these available[53] and would have wanted to, not only because he was a protector of Anguier, but also because he was an admirer of Poussin and was the one who had revived the project for the Grand Galerie between 1668 and 1674.[54]

Returning to the 'nude' state of Jean Pesne's engraving of *Pluto*, which belonged to Pierre II Mariette, as has already been noted, it is signed and dated 1692 and is in the *Réserve* of the Cabinet des Estampes, although filed under 'Gérard Audran'. Also in the *Réserve*, filed correctly under 'Pesne', is a complete set of the suite of engravings of the *Travaux d'Hercule* (as contained in the volume offered by Anguier to the *Académie*) but *in folio* and lacking the legends. What is of particular interest is that this *Réserve* suite also belonged to Pierre II Mariette[55] who signed each plate, including the frontispiece (Plate 15) dating them in a manner identical to his signature and date on the *Pluto* engraving.[56] Obviously, the Pesne engravings were all acquired by him the same year, probably at the same time, and the inference is that they might all date back to the same period.[57]

It is difficult to imagine that Pesne would have engraved the figure of *Pluto* after Anguier died. Furthermore, an association of Pesne's *Hercules* suite of 1678 with his engraving of *Pluto* is implicit in several ways: because of the former's dedication to Michel Anguier and because of the subject matter, related to the sculptor's *conférences* with their particular emphasis on these two gods. A study of the very limited literature on Pesne's *oeuvre* shows that he specialised in engravings after paintings and drawings and almost never after sculpture. It seems realistic, therefore, to date his rare engraving of *Pluto* circa 1678, the period when Pesne's admiration for Michel Anguier is most evident and in which the *Hercules* suite was conceived by the engraver as an *hommage* and an appropriate tribute to the lifelong works of a great sculptor.

A feature which must be stressed here is that Pesne's engraving of *Pluto* is obviously drawn with a viewpoint looking *down*, thus eliminating the possibility that this could be the illustration of a statue, such as the Saint-Mandé stone version, and demonstrating that it is the engraving of a statuette. In confirmation of this, compare the many engravings, by many artists, depicting the life-size, or larger than life, statues in the park of Versailles. They are all drawn with a viewpoint from below, which conveys their monumental scale and which, in any case, would be the only practical method (Plate 18).[58]

At this point, one must consider the possibility that Pesne was using a terracotta model of *Pluto* or a bronze version for his source. Charpentier, in the *Galerie de Girardon*, illustrated a terracotta *modèle*, but only as part of a whole collection forming a *tableau*. However, there are important variations between Pesne and Charpentier which cannot be ignored and which indicate that the former artist was not following the same source as Charpentier.[59] As far as a bronze version is concerned, the literature does not present any evidence that a large and detailed bronze of the god was available prior to 1700 and the small bronze casts which are accepted as seventeenth century would hardly have been considered sufficiently important or detailed enough for an engraving.[60]

Considering the art of engraving sculptures, Florent Le Comte wrote in 1699 on the manner of representing free-standing sculptures, alone and without background, noting that such sculptures were 'generally made either of stone or white marble, materials without any colour of their own'.[61] This suggests that, at that period, in France at least, it was not the practice to engrave single illustrations of, or after, terracotta or bronze statuettes. Elsewhere, in the seventeenth century, engravings after contemporaneous bronzes are known, e.g. the *Galleria Giustiniana*, which includes an engraving after a Duquesnoy bronze but only as part of a famous collection of antiquities. One searches in vain for a seventeenth-century French engraving which illustrates an *independent* bronze or terracotta statuette.[62] It must follow, therefore, that Pesne's engraving was of a marble statuette.

NOTES TO CHAPTER IV – numbers 41 to 62

41. Robert-Dumesnil, 1865, vol. IX, p. 314, no. 172. However, over the many years that he was compiling his Catalogue, the author overlooked the fact that in 1838 he had already given a third state of this engraving, un-lettered and uninscribed, correctly to Jean Pesne (Vol. III, p. 150, no. 50, which reads: '*Vulcain en avant de Cerbère. Le dieu est vu presque de face, portant la tête à droite, où il regarde; il tient sa barbe d'une main et s'appuie, de l'autre sur une fourche. Le fond est blanc. Morceau sans nom.')* This description under the title of '*Vulcain*' is unmistakably that of Pluto and Cerberus. Unfortunately, this engraving has apparently disappeared.

42. The signature 'G. *a*udran' is suspect. On most of his engravings, Audran signed his name 'G. Audran' or 'G. Audran sculp.', with the pointed classical Latin 'A'. Less frequently, he signed with a cursive capital '*a*', preceded by the abbreviation of his first name: 'Gir. *a*udran Sculps' followed by the year of the publication which, for this form of signature, we have found only 1680 and 1681 (Plate 18). Furthermore, the contemporaneous alternative spelling of Anguier is recorded (Bruel, p. 43) as 'Anguer' or 'Anguerre' but not as 'Anguiere'. Finally, Gérard Audran would certainly have known that there was no marble *Pluto* in Versailles.

43. Weigert, vol. I, p. 146, no. 181. Weigert's *Inventaire* does not go beyond the letter 'L', vol. 7. It is currently being continued by Maxime Préaud, *conservateur* at the Cabinet des Estampes, who published a two volume work on 'Leclerc' in 1980 and is now working on 'LePautre'. The letter 'P' (including 'Pesne') is not expected to be reached for many years. However, the *inventaire* of Claude Mellan was recently published out of sequence by Préaud to coincide with the exhibition given of that engraver at the Bibliothèque Nationale (see further, note 62).

44. For instance, plates by Jean Pesne, whose importance is demonstrated in this study, were purchased by Gérard Audran 'who retouched them with great judgement . . .' (Joseph Strutt, *A Biographical Dictionary of all the Engravers*, London, 1785, reprinted Geneva, 1972).

45. Robert-Dumesnil, vol. IX, p. 245. Also: Weigert, vol. I, pp. 124–125.

46. Pierre II Mariette's practice of signing and dating engravings in his collection is recorded by Lugt (no. 1788).

47. Dussieux, vol. I, pp. 449, 463.

48. Writers' translation of the Latin dedication (Plate 15). The abbreviation 'D.D.' stands for '*Dono Dedit*', 'given as a gift' (presented). 'D.C.Q.' means '*Dicat Consecrat Que*' or 'Conceived and dedicated by'.

    Robert-Dumesnil, vol. III, p. 145, quotes the full Latin dedication and lists in detail and with complete titles the eighteen Pesne engravings comprising the series of the *Travaux d'Hercule* (pp. 146–150).

49. This would be an explanation as to why the engraver chose Michel's *Pluto* as a subject for the engraving. Also, why he illustrated only this one god and not, for example, *Amphitrite*, *Neptune*, or any of the other gods and goddesses from Michel's suite. Another explanation could be that Pluto was the only god of whom the sculptor had carved a marble.

50. This bound set now in the Bibliothèque de l'Ecole des Beaux-Arts (no. 1332 A 3 – *Réserve*) contains the frontispiece and the series of eighteen engravings, *après la lettre*, with the names of the artists and the titles making up the legends. See also: Montaiglon, *Procès-verbaux*, vol. II, p. 150, *Le huit juillet 1679*. '*Monsieur Anguer fait présent d'un livre d'estempe contenant huit* (sic) *feille gravée sur les desseins de desfunt Mr Poussain sur les Travaux d'Hercule pour estre gardée en l'Académie*'. (After checking the manuscript itself, it was found that Montaiglon quoted the inaccurate number '*huit*' which was a slip originating in the *procès-verbal* which should have read '*dix-huit*' instead.)

51. Weigert, *La gravure et la renommée de Poussin*, p. 281. Imitating Louis XIV, private owners of works by Poussin were having engravings made of their paintings and distributing them to enhance their standing. 'This promoted the successful career of Jean Pesne, considered one of the best and most faithful engravers of Poussin'.

52. A. Blunt, 1951, p. 370. At the end of 1640, Poussin arrived in Paris commissioned by Louis XIII and Richelieu, through Sublet des Noyers, *Surintendant des bâtiments du Roi*, to design the decoration of the Grande Galerie of the Louvre. The project was never executed beyond the drawing stage (p. 373) as Poussin left in discontent for Rome in 1642, never to return to Paris. Work was however carried on but without energy and, after the retirement of des Noyers in 1643, was finally abandoned. Nevertheless (p. 375) 'the project exercised a considerable influence on artists of the next generation and more particularly (cf. Germain Brice) sculptors who considered it as a school from which they drew inspiration and ideas which served them infinitely'.

53. The drawings were in the possession of the *Surintendance des bâtiments du Roi* and were therefore available to Colbert.

54. A. Blunt, 1951, p. 373. Saint-Aymour, pp. 18, 19, 206. About 1668, Colbert revived the project by commissioning Louis de Boullongne *le vieux* (1609–1674) to repair fire damage done to a part of what had been executed and to continue the undertaking. Assisted successively by his elder son, Bon, and then by the younger, Louis, progress was made uninterruptedly until 1674 when the scheme was again abandoned with the death of Louis de Boullongne. The *Comptes des bâtiments du Roi* record that payments were made regularly during those years. The whole decoration was finally destroyed when the Grand Galerie was transformed into a museum in the 1780s.

55. For the *Hercule* series owned by Pierre II Mariette, cf. *Réserve* of the Cabinet des

Estampes, Ed. 47a, folio 24, et seq. In his manuscript *Abécédario*, Pierre-Jean Mariette wrote about the collection of engravings which he had inherited from his family and included much valuable information from his grandfather. Unfortunately, the pages relating to Jean Pesne (which are listed under the letter 'P' in Pierre-Jean's own index to vol. V) have been missing for over a century. Consequently, such information as might have existed on the *Pluto* engraving is not available. The *Inventaire après décès* of Pierre II (Arch. nat., Min. centr., XXIII – 426) has been consulted; it consists mainly of household property.

It should be noted that the association between Jean Pesne and Pierre II Mariette extended over a long period. One can cite, for example, his engraved portrait of François Langlois, after the well-known painting by Van Dyck which was commissioned after Langlois' death in 1647 and bears Pierre II's '*excudit*'. (*Réserve* of the Cabinet des Estampes, Ed. 47a, folio 55). François Langlois, called 'Ciartres', (1589–1647), a famous *marchand d'estampes*, well-connected throughout Europe, musician and *bon vivant*, traded in Paris under the sign '*Aux colonnes d'Hercule*'. Pierre II Mariette married his widow in 1655, thus amalgamating his own business with that of '*Aux colonnes d'Hercule*'. (Ref.: Weigert, *Les deux premiers Mariette et François Langlois*, p. 179).

56. For two of these engravings, again see Plates 16 and 17.

57. Apropos this, Robert-Dumesnil, in the 1838 catalogue, listed Pesne's *oeuvre* in what he judged to be chronological order. The '*Vulcain/Pluto*' engraving entry directly follows those for the suite of the *Travaux d'Hercule* which, of course, is dated 1678.

58. The repudiated 'Audran' inscription on the 'fig-leaf' engraving of *Pluto* refers to a statue '*Dix pieds de haut*'. This is well over three metres high, which seems exaggerated or based on ignorance. Michel's stone gods at Saint-Mandé were approximately 2.15 m to 2.60 m high, for example. In any case, the scale given in the inscription does not correspond to a subject drawn with a viewpoint from above.

59. In Pesne's engraving, besides Pluto's differently-shaped fork and, as in the present marble, the god's hairless genitalia, Cerberus has a thick, curly coat while in Charpentier's he appears smooth-skinned. In Pesne, the tail, which is also thick-haired, flops over the side of the drawn base in two distinct locks, again as in the marble group, whereas, in the other engraving, it is clear that the tail passes forward, over the rear paw, with the end tucked away under the animal's body. This would suggest different models for Pesne and, several years later, Charpentier (compare Plates 9 and 14).

60. Refer Appendix B, on the various bronze versions of the model.

61. Florent Le Comte, vol. I, p. 146, '*Sur la manière de représenter de la Sculpture*'.

62. The exhibition of Claude Mellan (1598–1688) at the Bibliothèque Nationale in Paris

(May–August 1988) and the concurrent publication of the Inventory of his engravings in the Département des Estampes (see note 33), supports the affirmation in this paragraph. Mellan engraved some twenty plates of the *Galleria Giustiniana* in Rome and subsequently, in Paris, the works of art in the *Cabinet du Roi*. The sculptures illustrated in each instance are marble antiquities, the only exception being two bronzes in the *Galleria* which were an antique statuette of *Hercules* and, exceptionally, the contemporaneous *Mercury* commissioned of Duquesnoy to be its pendant (ref. Metropolitan Museum of Art, 'Liechtenstein Princely Collections', N.Y. 1985, cat. no. 49, entry by Olga Raggio). Although it is well documented that this *Mercury* was a bronze, it is catalogued by Préaud as a marble.

V

Michel Anguier's Marble Pluto: Comparison with Other Carvings

It has been demonstrated that Jean Pesne's engraving of Michel Anguier's *Pluto* logically dates back to about 1678 and that he illustrated a small marble which, at that date, would necessarily have been carved by Anguier himself. Obviously, the figure engraved by Pesne, in the context of his '*hommage*' to the master, cannot be considered a later work by another sculptor. Furthermore, as both the engraving and the marble represent Pluto completely nude, without pubic hair and with similar genitalia, and as no other contemporaneous representation is known offering the same observations, it does not seem excessive to affirm that the Pesne engraving, unknown in the literature on Michel Anguier, is after the present marble.[63]

Additional evidence is also available in establishing its paternity. From observation, this marble *Pluto* could be described in the following terms: 'it is of short and strong proportions, the expression on his face indicates melancholy, his flesh seems heavy, soft and damp, and his muscles appear plump . . .'. These, however, are the words (previously quoted on page 24) that Michel used to describe the *Pluto* which he had executed and to which he was pointing in his two *conférences* of 1669 and 1676. The present marble is a masterly carving, particularly considering its small scale,[64] which demonstrates all the characteristics which were being emphasised by the sculptor. These qualities explain why it earned the documented admiration of everyone who saw it at the *conférence* of 1669.

Its size, if apparently unprecedented for a marble sculpture by Michel Anguier, is appropriate for a work that needed to be easily moved (in fact, it is no heavier than a similar solid terracotta statuette) and it can be assumed that, if Michel did carve such a marble with that purpose in mind, he used it to demonstrate his theories at the *Académie*.[65]

In ascribing this marble figure to Michel Anguier, an examination of its stylistic relationship to other works by him is essential, although necessarily limited because of the few related marble or stone sculptures which survive. As has already been noted, there are only two marble carvings extant which can be given to the sculptor himself. His moving, life-size *Christ crucified, alive* in the Chapelle de la Vierge of the Church of Saint-Roch is a rarely-published carving (1684) and was his last major commission (Plates 37a and b).[66] His group of *The Nativity*, also in Saint-Roch (Plate 20), is more relevant for comparison because it is contemporaneous with *Pluto*. *The Nativity* was eulogised in 1983 by Germain Bazin of the Institut de France as a 'masterpiece of the world's sculpture'[67] and more recently (1989) by Jean-Pierre Babelon, the eminent historian of old Paris and Director of the Versailles Museum and its domain, who wrote 'rarely did the sculptors of the classic period attain such a depth of religious feeling'.[68] Although on a much larger scale than *Pluto*, it nevertheless includes the figure of St Joseph (Plate 21) which does offer the possibility of stylistic comparisons.[69] On both the Saint's and Pluto's head, the carving of the hair shows a striking resemblance, with short curls flowing with movement, taking root and parting in a like fashion (compare Plates 5 and 23 with 22, for instance). Also, importantly, the manner of carving the inside of certain curls should be observed: clearly visible within a central curl on the head of the Saint and mirrored inside a curl on the head of Pluto is a distinct ridge, or hard-edge 'step' which is a very particular treatment and may be considered autographic (again, compare Plates 23 and 24). In support of this, when a 'faithful' copy of the group was carved in 1869 to replace it in the Val-de-Grâce, to the same scale, the sculptor who carved it did not observe the interior of this curl in the same manner (Plate 22; Bazin 1983, illn. opp. p. 101 and caption).[70]

The largest group of carvings by Michel Anguier (albeit in stone rather than marble) which still exists *in situ* is the remarkable complex of reliefs which he executed on the command of the Queen, Anne d'Autriche, to decorate the Church of the Val-de-Grâce in Paris between 1662 and 1667. The carving of all the relief sculptures in this church by Michel himself is documented, having been fully noted by Guillet de Saint-Georges[71] and also described in detail by Henri Stein.[72] These include the four enormous *hauts-reliefs* of the Evangelists on the spandrels, partly in the round (diameter 3.5 m; Plates 25–31), which dominate the interior beneath the dome. Three of these display certain details of carving which are reflected in the marble *Pluto*: this time the movement of a beard, its short curls flowing almost horizontally (compare Saint Mark, Plate 26 and Plates 5 and 23), the treatment of a finger (Saint Mark; Saint Luke, Plate 28; Saint Matthew, Plate 30) and certainly the emphasis on musculature and veining in arms, hands and legs, which is present even in a small carving like *Pluto* and clearly preoccupies the sculptor (again compare the three Saints and PLATES 1–4). The consistency is apparent. Of particular interest are also the two small allegorical reliefs of lambs high up on the arcade of the entrance to the Chapelle Saint-Louis (PLATE 32) in which the fur is sketched in sure and simple strokes of the tool (PLATES 33, 34) which may be compared with the shorter hair on Cerberus' hind quarters (PLATES 4 and 45). Compare as well the peculiar shape of ears on the lamb (PLATE 33) and on the left-hand head at the back of Cerberus (PLATES 4 and 39).

In addition to stylistic comparisons, scientific support has also been forthcoming: two separate analyses of the rock material from which *Pluto* and *The Nativity* were carved, reveal that it is the same marble. Furthermore, as is explained in Appendix C, the two sets of data are indeed so close that the conclusion follows that the two sculptures derived, in all probability, from the same block.

The significance of this, taken in conjunction with the unmistakeable affinity of style and technique between the marble *Pluto* and other carved works by Michel, and the contemporaneous documentation provided by the two *conférences* cited, as well as by the Jean Pesne engraving, clearly demonstrates that this marble figure is from the hand of Michel Anguier, dating back to before 1669, the year that he displayed it at the *Académie* during his first *conférence*.

NOTES TO CHAPTER V – numbers 63 to 72

63. Only one aspect of comparison between Pesne's engraving and the marble *Pluto* cannot be resolved: the shape of the base. Pesne's base appears to be uneven and may, or may not, exactly represent the original form. As the marble base was reshaped in the eighteenth century, there is no way of ascertaining that it originally conformed to Pesne's observation. However, compare Cerberus' tail and the manner in which it flops over the base in both the engraving and the marble (PLATES 2 and 44 with 14). The details are identical, as is the position of the animal's rump in relation to the edge (PLATES 1 and 14).

64. The scale is unusual for the period in France and this carving of *Pluto*, despite the restraints of a comparitively small block of marble, shows exceptional ability and confidence on the part of the sculptor. It could be said to anticipate the later *morceaux de réception*, in the round, which were original marble sculptures of small dimensions, executed after subjects imposed by the *Académie*, and required from sculptors to demonstrate their skill in solving technical and artistic problems, before their admittance into that institution.

65. Although it was not a common practice in France before the eighteenth century, there was an ongoing tradition in that country of small carved marble figures, mostly religious in subject matter. By the early seventeenth century, such figures began to be considered sufficiently intimate and self-contained to be placed in a *cabinet* and Marthe Digard has noted that with Jacques Sarrazin's two statuettes of *St Peter* (height, 63 cm) and *St Mary-Magdalen* (height, 56 cm), both now in the Louvre, 'religious art adapted itself to the small scale of apartments' (*Jacques Sarrazin*, Paris 1934, p. 186).

It must also be remembered that Michel Anguier had spent several years in Italy and was familiar with small, secular marble statuettes, even if many of his French contemporaries were not. It is easy to imagine that the demonstration, in 1669, of a small, finely-carved figure such as *Pluto* before the *Académie* would have created a very strong impression.

66. Its dimensions, communicated by M. G. Brunel, Cons. en chef du Service des églises de Paris, are: h. 2.30 m, w. 1.75 m, d. 0.45 m. Due to its perilous condition, the chapel in which the marble *Christ* is housed has been closed to the public for a long time. Earlier illustrations of the installation show a bizarre period in its history when J.-B. II Lemoyne's poignant, kneeling figure of Mignard's daughter, the Comtesse de Feuquières (from the painter's ravaged tomb) was recruited to act as Magdalen at the foot of Anguier's crucifix. Happily, she again kneels by Lemoyne's bust of her father in another part of the church.

67. Bazin, p. 104: '*C'est un chef-d'oeuvre de la sculpture mondiale . . .*'.

68. Babelon, p. 75: '*Rarement les sculpteurs de l'époque classique ont atteint à une telle profondeur du sentiment religieux.*'

69. A master does not change his style because he works on a larger or smaller scale and his small sculptures are only small in size, not in artistic stature. The difference in a small carving is the need for greater technical ability, using finer tools, yet retaining his individuality.

70. The sculptor who carved Saint Joseph was Louis-Antoine Desprey (1832–1892). Two other sculptors, Clément Denis (d. 1870) and Justin-Marie Lequien (1796–1881), each carved one of the other two figures in the group.

71. Dussieux, vol. I, pp. 442–444.

72. Stein, pp. 39–45.

APPENDIX A

Michel Anguier's Involvement in the Gardens of Versailles: Setting the Record Straight

PIERRE FRANCASTEL, in *La Sculpture de Versailles*, states quite clearly that there is no way of knowing if any sculptors were involved in the interior decoration of the château (or *pavillon de chasse*) built under Louis XIII. As for the exterior of the building and the park, there definitely was no work of art to be seen. It is only in the first years of the personal reign of Louis XIV (subsequent to Fouquet's fall in 1661) that sculpture was introduced. Actually, however, work in Versailles between 1661 and 1663 consisted almost exclusively of the transformation of Louis XIII's château, before any new arrangement for the park. It was only after 1664, when Colbert was named *Surintendant des bâtiments du Roi*, that the first significant works made their appearance, for which records were consistently kept from then on. The first sculptural decorations consisted mostly of mythological terms and architectural vases executed by the *Sculpteurs ordinaires des bâtiments du Roi* who were referred to as the sculptors of the *Maîtrise*. These included, among others, Anguier, Buyster, Lerambert and Magnier. We know that there were forty-seven terms adorning the park before 1666 and that six, according to Guillet de Saint-Georges, were commissioned from Michel Anguier to decorate the original central alley. They were probably never put into place because of the decision, shortly afterwards, to widen the walk and to adopt a new programme for the decorations. There were also eight stone statues larger than life-size by Lerambert and Buyster at the far end of the park and around the large *rondeau*. These remained in place until 1693, but the terms, which were also made of stone, were either destroyed during the renovations or taken to Paris where they eventually crumbled away, before the end of the century. From 1664, the park developed very rapidly until 1666 when it seems to have come to a dead-end for several reasons: the lack of a sense of direction and a need for coordination between the *Maîtrise* and the *Académie*, as well as the failure to meet the grandiose designs of the King.

From then on, a new and decisive orientation took place under the doctrine of the *Académie*, with Le Brun firmly in charge. Rational plans began to evolve for the progressive 'invasion' of all the perspectives of the park by sculptures, either original or after the antique. The main achievements between 1666 and 1669, which included no additional contribution by Michel Anguier, were concentrated in the park itself, with its gardens, fountains, vistas and canals, and also with the arrival of the first truly great works characteristic of Versailles. The various elements of the whole sculptural ensemble, already conceived in 1666, did not however begin to reach completion before 1672, resulting in the overall transformation of Louis XIII's domanial grounds. This early period is usually referred to as that of *le premier décor* of the gardens of Versailles. By 1672, also, new allegorical sculptures were added on the east side façade of the early château, still visible today, while mythological embellishments were already under way in the interior. This led to the decision, just before 1674, to integrate the symbolism that had emerged with a new sculpture programme for the park. A very important order for twenty-eight over life-size marble sculptures, known as the *Grande Commande*, was commissioned by Colbert to be executed, after designs by Le Brun, by major sculptors of the *Académie*, but without the participation of Michel Anguier. It was not, however, until after the 1680s that these sculptures were put into place when the park had undergone various reorganisations. The palace itself was then to reach new proportions and the interior to obtain new decors, always in conformity with the designs of the *Académie* and the wishes of the King.

Although widely asserted, until comparatively recently, that Anguier's *Pluto* was a large marble figure standing in the gardens of Versailles, this mistaken opinion has now been discarded. There are no receipts for it nor any mention of it in the *Comptes des bâtiments du Roi*. Certainly, Thomassin's engravings of all the sculptures in the park in 1694 do not include such a figure. Furthermore, if such a major marble had existed, it would undoubtedly have been mentioned by Guillet de Saint-Georges in his *Mémoire* of 1690. Also, if this marble figure of *Pluto* was indeed in the park of Versailles earlier, it seems unlikely that an important work by a major sculptor such as Michel would just simply disappear. Following the Desplaces engravings, similar errors were perpetuated for a marble *Ceres* and a marble *Neptune* in the park at Versailles. In fact, the only large figure by the sculptor which ever stood there was his *Amphitrite* although this was carved by a *praticien* between 1680 and 1684 (see note 1), probably under Michel's supervision, and installed in the Bosquet des Dômes.

One of the reasons for Michel Anguier's minimal involvement in Versailles, at least where its early years are concerned, seems apparent: Guillet de Saint-Georges confirms that between 1662 and 1667 his time was mainly taken up with the extraordinary commission from Queen Anne d'Autriche, for all the sculptures in the Val-de-Grâce. Also, Guillet continues, Michel executed in 1663 two large stone figures of Saints for the Church of the Pères de la Merci. In 1664, he carved the six mythological terms for Versailles, mentioned earlier; in 1667, he did the decorations commissioned by Colbert for the Chapel dedicated to Matrimony in the Church of Saint-Eustache; in 1668, there were other, apparently unspecified, works for Colbert and, at the end of that year, there was the stucco bas-relief for the main altar at Saint-Denis de Chartres. In 1669, he carved the life-size stone statues of two Saints and two Angels for the main altar of the Church of the Filles-Dieu. The following year was the beginning of a new decade and we already know that it witnessed a decline in his activities except, between 1674 and 1676, when he carved the very handsome reliefs and sculptures of the Porte Saint-Denis (Plates 35–36) which Louis Gonse described as superior to any such arch built in modern times, whose invention was the rarest and most perfect in (French) architecture.[73] 'The carvings', he added, 'respond to the beauty of the arch and to the harmony of its proportions; in a restrained manner they achieve the most striking grandeur.'[74] Despite assertions in the literature that the initial designs for the decorations were by Le Brun, there are no recorded drawings by him in support of this theory. In fact, Lesueur clearly documents that all the decorations for the arch were conceived by Michel Anguier himself.[75] Thus, these offer further evidence of the sculptor's striking inventiveness, even in his later years.

As far as these years are concerned, particularly after 1667, when he had completed the extensive sculptural decoration of the Val-de-Grâce, which had been commissioned independently of Le Brun's authority, one of the reasons for his lack of commissions for one or more sculptures for Versailles can be explained, as has previously been noted, by the long-standing conflict of personalities between the two artists. As Dean Walker has already suggested,[76] Le Brun had several reasons to be displeased with Michel Anguier: his resistance to Le Brun's rise to power in the 1660s, his rejection, along with Mignard, of an offer of reconciliation and, above all, his independent spirit which would have particularly antagonised Le Brun. We have seen (Chapter III) that Anguier did join the *Académie* in 1668 to participate in a series of *conférences* but Mignard steadfastly refused to do so until Le Brun's death in 1690. Ironically, he took over as director and succeeded Le Brun in all his functions.

NOTES TO APPENDIX A – numbers 73 to 76

73. Gonse, p. 171.

74. op. cit., also p. 171: '*La décoration répond à la beauté du plan, à l'harmonie des proportions; avec des moyens discrets elle atteint à la plus saisissante grandeur.*'

75. Lesueur, p. 189. It has also been suggested by several writers, starting with Germain Brice in 1687, up to as recently as 1985, that François Anguier also worked on the Porte Saint-Denis. This is palpably wrong: François Anguier died in 1669, some years before the Arch was commissioned.

76. Walker, p. 178 and note 223.

APPENDIX B

Some Observations on the Various Bronze Versions of the Model

The present study of the marble *Pluto* by Michel Anguier would not be complete without a brief consideration of the various bronze versions of the model, nor without some notice of a terracotta version which has been brought to our attention.

The known bronzes of *Pluto* all follow Michel's invention with no significant changes in the composition, the differences being attributable to the intervention of different *bronziers* at different periods and to the varying success of their modellers in interpreting Michel's original figure. The bronzes may be divided into two distinct categories: the smaller casts, which are less than 25 cm high, are not numerous and, generally speaking, are earlier in period; and the larger and more decorative casts, which are about 55 cm high, even fewer in number and were probably executed in the eighteenth century.[77] None of the published bronze versions of *Pluto*, or of any of the other gods and goddesses in the suite, has ever been convincingly identified as one of the original mid-seventeenth-century casts made for Monsieur de Montarsis. As was mentioned in Chapter III, the Comte de Caylus, who had apparently seen these, wrote that there was 'nothing marvellous' about them.

The earliest, securely dateable bronze cast of *Pluto* is that acquired for Augustus the Strong in 1699 which is in the Grünes Gewölbe in Dresden (PLATE 46). It is 24.5 cm high and, given Augustus' importance as a collector, it is puzzling that this cast, purchased in Paris by the Elector's artistic adviser, the French architect Raymond LePlat, is on this small scale which is half the height of the original 1652 model (48.6 cm). Given that the same collection contains a fine and large bronze of Michel's *Mars* (h. 54.5 cm; Washington, 1978, cat. no. 510, illustrated), the conclusion must be drawn that no such large cast of *Pluto* was available to Monsieur LePlat. The Dresden *Pluto* has been illustrated by Weihrauch and Wardropper, among others, but such illustrations are poor and rob it of its character.[78] In fact, on examination, one is immediately struck by its high quality and it is not out of place in that extraordinary collection; for its size, the musculature is adequately defined and the extremities well-articulated while the patination is a rich medal brown.[79] Nevertheless, to accept such a small, posthumous bronze as a faithful representation of Michel's original *Pluto* seems extravagant. A similar, recently-published cast (h. 23.5 cm) in Kassel (PLATE 47) is the only example known to us depicting the god without a fig-leaf, as in the marble. It is documented as in the collection of the Landgraves of Hessen-Kassel by 1767, having originally been purchased on the assumption that it was Hercules.[80] Other small casts (e.g. the Cleveland *Pluto*, h. 23.5 cm[81]) which have had their period related to that of the well-documented Dresden cast cannot be compared to it in facture or quality. At least one small cast exists without Cerberus.[82]

It seems reasonable to compare the present marble with one of the few large and detailed bronzes known of the model – in fact, the only cast in this category accessible at this time. This is the *Pluto* now to be seen in the Bouvier Collection of the Musée Carnavalet in Paris (PLATES 48–50). This bronze and its pendant are generally accepted to be Louis XIV period[83] and they were probably in a Paris auction sale by 1775.[84] The size of the bronze *Pluto* (54 cm), as well as its quality, presumably allows the character of Michel's original invention to be more convincingly translated than in the smaller casts. A careful comparison of it with the marble *Pluto* shows such a close resemblance that it is conceivable that it derives from this very sculpture. The bronze, however, does not reproduce the subtle observation of the finely carved marble: for instance, *Pluto*'s hair is sketchily defined, the musculature is simplified and Cerberus' coat is less textured (PLATE 48). Nevertheless, it is interesting to note that this bronze reflects (as, indeed, do the Dresden and other bronze versions) the flat back of Cerberus' body, a distinctive feature presumably imposed upon the sculptor by the dimensions of the original block of marble (PLATES 2 and 50).

Any study of the *Pluto* bronzes will show that ignorance of the original sculptor of the figure was prevalent by the mid-eighteenth century. Hubert Landais has observed 'The *Neptune* and *Amphitrite* are the only statuettes listed by Guillet de Saint-Georges accepted in the eighteenth century as the work of Anguier'.[85] This would explain why the Carnavalet *Pluto* is not paired with another of the suite of Michel's gods but with a reduction[86] after the antique marble of *Silenus and the infant Bacchus*, which was in the French royal collections.

For some time a terracotta version of *Pluto* has been known which is in a private collection and has never been published. It was in Paris in 1961, when it was cited in an entry for a bronze *Pluto* which was included in the '*Louis XIV – Faste et Décor*' exhibition at the Musée des Arts Décoratifs.[87] This terracotta, which is now in New

York, is attributed to Michel Anguier and measures 54 cm in height.[88] This is neither the reported height of the original model for M. de Montarsis (48.6 cm) nor the estimated height of the terracotta *modèle* belonging to Girardon (about 75 cm). The New York terracotta cannot be a *moulage* of the present marble, being one-third smaller, nor is it likely that it could be another *modèle* for it. However, its size is similar to that of the Carnavalet bronze, suggesting the possibility that the terracotta was modelled preliminary to the casting of this, or another, eighteenth-century bronze of the same dimensions.[89] If so, as the Carnavalet example reflects the marble *Pluto*, it would follow that the terracotta version was modelled after the present sculpture and this hypothesis would tend to be confirmed if the terracotta Cerberus displays the distinctive flat back of the marble dog, referred to above.

NOTES TO APPENDIX B – numbers 77 to 89

77. When discussing the numerous bronzes of *Amphitrite*, Fischer also observed that the smaller casts of the goddess (about 30 cm high) appeared to be the earlier examples. (Fischer, no. 20)

78. Holzhausen (p. 165, fig. 5) and Weihrauch (p. 399, fig. 483) used the identical, pre-1939 photograph of this bronze. Wardropper's illustration (plate X, fig. 16) shows the painted inventory number '58' which it had been given by 1976.

79. The Dresden *Pluto* is presently kept in the reserves of the Albertinum and we are most grateful to Dipl. phil. Martin Raumschüssel, Director of the Skulpturensammlung, for giving us the opportunity of examining this bronze and discussing it with him; also for providing the photograph to illustrate it in this study.

80. Kassel, p. 282, no. 542, illustrated. This bronze statuette was the subject of a paper given by the Landgrave Frederic II of Hessen-Kassel (r. 1760–1785) to the Société des Antiquités in 1767. In it, he proposed that the figure was not of Hercules but of Pluto, God of the Underworld. The change of identity must have been disappointing in a city which, since the early eighteenth century, has been dominated by a creation of the Landgrave Carl (r. 1670–1730), the 72 metre high 'Herkulesmonument' on the heights of Wilhelmshöhe, a gigantic (over 9 metres) copper version of the Hercules Farnese atop the pyramid-shaped roof of an octagonal pavilion, itself sited above an elaborate rococo cascade descending the hillside below. But there were several other figures of Hercules in the collections, to compensate for this loss.

81. This cast, which is illustrated in the Cleveland Museum *Bulletin* of June 1982, p. 167, has been examined by the authors.

82. Rijksmuseum, Amsterdam, in whose catalogue this bronze is given to François Anguier (Leeuwenberg, p. 423, no. 740, illustrated).

83. Madame Henriette Bouvier willed her collection to the Musée Carnavalet in 1965. It went on exhibition in 1968 and a documented catalogue was published shortly afterwards. Madeleine Charageat, sister of Marguerite Charageat, was Curator at Carnavalet until her retirement in 1963 but remained Consultant to the museum for several years after. Presumably, she supervised the Bouvier catalogue entry for the bronze *Pluto* and its pendant *Silenus*, describing both of them as 'Louis XIV or eighteenth century' (Ville de Paris, *Collection Henriette Bouvier léguée au Musée Carnavalet*, Paris, n.d., nos. 21, 22).

Apropos the Carnavalet cast, it is worth adding that the only other bronze version of *Pluto* comparable in scale and period which can be cited here, is the cast which was in the Olsen Art Collection, called 'Neptune' in the catalogue, with *Amphitrite*, called 'Venus', as pendant (H. Schmitz, *De Olsen Art Collection*, Munich

1924, nos. 786, 787, height 55 cm, illustrated). Here *Pluto* is shown with a drape, similar to that in the Desplaces engraving, but held in his right hand in a distinct variation from the original model. The bronze cast referred to in note 87, also 55 cm in height, may belong to this group.

84. This pair of bronzes, or two similar casts, were in the Caulet d'Hautville sale in 1775, the catalogue describing Pluto as '*Hercule vainqueur de Cerbère*'. Ref.: Charles Blanc, *Trésor de la Curiosité*, Paris 1857, vol. I, pp. 252–253.

85. Landais (1968) was examining, particularly, Paris sales catalogue descriptions of the mid to late eighteenth century in a review of the exhibition 'The French Bronze'.

86. Illustrated (opp. no. 6) in the Bouvier catalogue cited in note 83. A terracotta reduction, 55 cm high, of *Silenus and the infant Bacchus*, patinated to simulate bronze, was sold in Paris, Palais Galliera, 24 March 1969, lot no. 251.

87. The bronze *Pluto* (height given as 55 cm) was not illustrated in the catalogue. Its pendant was Michel's *Neptune*, although the two casts were catalogued individually. (Ref. '*Louis XIV – Faste et Décor*', Musée des Arts Décoratifs, Paris, May–October 1960, nos. 700, 701.)

88. Written communication from Professor Thomas Hedin.

89. As, for example, the terracotta *Silenus* referred to above in note 86.

APPENDIX C

The Conclusion of Two Isotopic Analyses: One Marble for Pluto and The Nativity

In writing the study of the marble *Pluto* by Michel Anguier, one essential aspect of its execution has not been touched upon. This is the variety and the source of the marble block from which the figure was carved. In any consideration of the availability of fine white statuary marble to a French sculptor in the seventeenth century, it must be accepted that this 'noble' material was a luxury not easily obtained, even by a master. Normally, the importance of a commission and the finances available for it might ensure that such marble or marbles as were needed for a project would be selected, possibly by the sculptor himself travelling to the chosen quarry or by an agent of the patron for whom the commission was to be executed. The preference might be for marble from Carrara,[90] whose white rock had (and still has) an unrivalled reputation for purity but other quarries, including Saint-Béat in the Pyrénées,[91] also offered white marble of almost comparable quality. The process of selecting and purchasing the marble at the quarry, the transportation of often huge blocks by primitive methods, to the final delivery to the sculptor's studio was a long, arduous and costly proposition.

It has been deduced that *Pluto* was not a commissioned work but was carved by Michel for his own purposes – particularly, to demonstrate his theories on the interplay of emotions and anatomy. The question therefore arises: would he have been able to afford a piece of fine statuary marble for his own use and how would such a block be available? It will be recalled that a date of before 1669 has been established for *Pluto*. This was shortly after Michel's involvement in the Church of the Val-de-Grâce, in which the most important single work was the marble group of *The Nativity* for the main altar, commissioned by Queen Anne d'Autriche and intended, as indeed was the entire church, as a pious demonstration of her gratitude at the birth, some years earlier, of her son, the future Louis XIV. Because of the extent of his work in the Val-de-Grâce, it seems unlikely that Michel would have been free to travel and to select the original block of marble for the group himself and it was probably ordered for him, either by the Queen's agents or through the auspices of the *Surintendance des bâtiments du Roi*.

The original block of marble for *The Nativity* from the quarry would have to have been very large as the overall dimensions of the final group are more than 4 metres wide and 1.6 metres high, with a maximum depth of almost 1 metre.[92] Certainly, it was cut into three sections to facilitate its transportation to Paris, the largest section being that intended for Saint Joseph. It is documented that it became the practice in the seventeenth century for the blocking-out stage (i.e. the reduction of a block to a closer approximation of the ultimate sculpture) to be achieved in the sculptor's studio[93] and, presumably, this was the case with the three sub-divided blocks of marble for *The Nativity*.

The coincidence of Michel Anguier having worked on this, his largest marble sculpture, and of having executed the marble *Pluto* quite shortly afterwards, sparked an admittedly optimistic hypothesis: could the small statuette have been carved from a piece of the unused marble, retained from his execution of *The Nativity*? The possibility was a long shot but it was decided to make a determined attempt to ascertain the variety of each of the two marble sculptures, its characteristics and, if possible, its origin. Accordingly, the Centre de Recherches sur les Monuments Historiques of the Ministère de la Culture in Paris was approached to ask if it was feasible for an analysis to be made of the marble fabric of Michel's group in the Church of Saint-Roch. This could not have been achieved without the assistance of Mme Annie Blanc of the Centre de Recherches who found the idea unprecedented and intriguing: documentation, even on major white marble sculptures in France, can be extensive or limited but, even in the first instance, it is often the case that the actual variety and source of the marble used is not recorded.

The experiment commenced, therefore, at the Church of Saint-Roch in Paris, in December 1989, when Mme Blanc, after obtaining the necessary authorisation, took the required tiny samples of marble from the back of the base of the figure of Saint Joseph from *The Nativity*, in the presence of a representative of the City of Paris, the titular owner of the group. Of the three separate elements of the group, Saint Joseph was selected for the test samples, arbitrarily, presuming that its size and projections would have offered the largest unused pieces of marble in the blocking-out process.

The fragments were sent by Mme Blanc to Professor R. Letolle of the Laboratoire de Biogéochimie Isotopique of the Université Pierre et Marie Curie for an identification of the rock, using stable isotope analysis, the application of which in the identification of white statuary marble is relatively recent.[94] Professor Letolle's result from this analytical procedure gave exact isotopic readings, placing the source of the marble used for Saint Joseph on the edge of an isotopic 'map' of Carrara[95] and closely relating to the Carrara 'signature' indicated by a data base for the Tuscan quarry.[96]

In London, in January 1990, permission was sought from the British Museum Research Laboratory for a complementary analysis of the marble of *Pluto*, informing them of the Paris test of the previous month and its result. The Keeper of the Laboratory, Dr Sheridan Bowman, gave her authorisation and, following the recommendation of Keith Matthews, who has been conducting isotopic analyses at the Research Laboratory, Anne Brodrick of the V & A Sculpture Conservation Department obtained two samples of marble powder from the underside of the figure of *Pluto* – one under the god's left foot and the other under Cerberus' rump. These two samples were passed on to Keith Matthews who analysed them individually, resulting in isotopic readings almost identical to that for Michel's Saint Joseph in Paris.[97] The three sets of data, shown on a graphic prepared by Mr Matthews, coincide to a startling degree (refer graphic in the B.M.R.L. report, following the present appendix: *Pluto* as '1' and '2', Saint Joseph as '3').

The striking similarity in the analyses of these two marble sculptures was unexpected and informative. It provides significant support for the preceding art-historical demonstration that *Pluto* was carved by Michel Anguier, which was written before the two analyses and, furthermore, offers scientific evidence indicating that he used a piece of marble retained during the execution of *The Nativity*. The data strongly suggests that the marble derived from Carrara although it cannot be conclusive in itself.[98] What is more important, for the present purpose, is the relationship that has been established between the marble fabric of Michel's masterpiece and that of *Pluto*. As was pointed out in London, the interpretation of the readings obtained from the analyses indicates that the two sculptures, independently tested, derived from marble, not just from the same quarry but 'from the same block'. The data from the London tests was conveyed to Paris, who also found the similarity astonishing. The enthusiasm of these two institutions over the results is understandable: they have been working on the application of isotope analysis to the identification of archeological material only – antique white marble sculptures, sarcophagi and monuments, often fragmentary. It is innovative in both countries to use this analytical procedure to identify marble from a non-archeological, i.e. post-antique, source. It was remarked that the matching readings were 'what one hopes for when trying to relate a disembodied antique head to a headless torso'.

Thus, given that there remains a need to establish a more complete library of data bases for quarries from which statuary marble has been excavated in the past, the application of isotope analysis offers the possibility of an important new contribution to the identification of modern white marble sculptures and to their authentication.

Appendix C

STABLE ISOTOPE ANALYSIS REPORT

by
Keith J. Matthews
British Museum Research Laboratory
22 February 1990

Report on the stable isotope analysis of a marble statuette of Pluto sculpted by Michel Anguier.

1.0 Introduction.

During the period 1665-67 the French sculptor Michel Anguier was commissioned to carve a marble monument depicting The Holy Family. This famous sculpture, which is larger than life-size is now in the Church of Saint Roch in Paris. In 1669 he carved, apparently without any commission, a statuette, about 73 cm tall, of Pluto and Cerberus. The owners of this statuette, whilst researching the history of Anguier's work, considered that it may have been carved from a small remnant from the block used for the earlier, much larger monument. It was believed that stable isotope analysis might confirm this hypothesis.

A sample from The Holy Family monument had previously been analysed in Paris by Professor Rene Letolle with the intention of determining the origin of its marble, but because the statuette was in England (undergoing restoration) it was opportune to have a sample taken from it and analysed at The British Museum. Accordingly, the owners, Mr Bernard Black and M Hugues-W Nadeau, submitted two samples taken from the base for analysis.

2.0 Experimental procedure.

The samples were obtained from the statuette by drilling: this operation was performed by Anne Brodrick of The Victoria and Albert Museum, London. The initial drillings were discarded, as per the normal procedure, in order to negate the possibility of analysing marble that has been isotopically modified by weathering or cleaning. From the resulting powder, 10 mg was reacted with 100% orthophosphoric acid under vacuum (McCrea, 1950). The carbon dioxide thus obtained was isotopically analysed using a VG Micromass 602D mass-spectrometer. The isotopic ratio (δ) obtained is given in parts per mil (‰ i.e. per thousand) relative to the PDB standard (Craig, 1957), where

$$\delta = \frac{(Rsample - Rpdb) \times 1000}{Rpdb} \text{‰}$$

and R= 13C/12C or 18O/16O

Each gas regeneration was performed twice to provide replicate samples; the standard error on these measurements is typically $\pm$ 0.05 ‰.

3.0 Results.

The results are given in the table, and are plotted graphically as the carbon isotope ratio δ13C versus the oxygen isotope ratio δ18O. Also on the plot are the 90% ellipses (Leese, 1988) of isotopic signatures obtained from data very kindly made available by Professor Norman Herz of the University of Georgia, (see also Herz, 1987). The Carrara data have been supplemented with results obtained by the British Museum laboratory. The ellipses selected include those for some of the more important marble quarrying areas in antiquity, and for which data are available, albeit limited.

4.0 Discussion.

The purpose of the analysis was to assess whether or not the two sculptures i.e. The Holy Family and Pluto with Cerberus were carved of the same marble. The two pairs of replicate results for the latter, obtained by this laboratory, are identical when experimental errors have been taken into account. Accordingly a mean result for the two samples is given in the table. If this mean result is compared with the result obtained by the French analysts for The Holy Family sculpture, it can be seen that there is no difference in the carbon ratios and a difference of only 0.12 ‰ in the oxygen ratios. It has to be emphasised that the assumption has been made that the French analysts have announced their results in parts per mil relative to the PDB standard (Craig, 1957).

Coleman and Walker (1979) experimented on sarcophagi, measuring isotope ratios of samples of sarcophagi taken from opposite sides of large sarcophagi i.e. about 2 metres apart on a single block. They found that for certain types of marble, the variation in isotopic ratios was about 0.1 ‰. In the case under consideration, because the isotopic differences in the marble of the two sculptures are so small, it is probable that the two sculptures are carved of the same marble.

The question of provenance for the marble is more difficult to address. Inspection of the plot shows that the results lie on the edge of the Carrara ellipse. This is consistent with the description of the marble as being fine-grained, and it is known that the Carrara quarries were producing marble at the time that these sculptures were produced. However, there are also quarries in the Pyrenees that were producing marble in the seventeenth century. Unfortunately, there is a great paucity of comparative data for these French quarries, but from four measurements undertaken by this laboratory of marble from St Béat (a plot of these results is given for comparison), it is quite conceivable that the marble used for these sculptures could be French.

5.0 Synopsis

The results of stable isotope analysis of the marble of the statuette support the theory that it and the much larger sculpture depicting The Holy family are of the same marble. However, due to the isotopic similarities of Carrara and French marble, it is not possible to ascribe a source to the marble; either could have provided the marble.

Acknowledgements.

I am indebted to Professor Norman Herz of the University of Georgia, U.S.A. for making his database of marble quarry analyses available.

References

Coleman, M., and Walker, S., 1979, Stable isotope identification of Greek and Turkish marbles, Archaeometry, 21, 107-112.

Craig, H., 1957, Isotopic standards for carbon and oxygen and correction factors for mass spectrometric analysis of CO2, Geochim. Cosmochim. Acta, 12, 133-149.

Herz, N., 1987, Carbon and oxygen isotopic ratios: a data base for classical Greek and Roman marble, Archaeometry, 29. 35-43.

Leese, M.N., 1988, Statistical treatment of stable isotope data, in Classical marble: geochemistry, technology, trade, Herz, N., and Waelkens, M., eds, Kluwer, Dordrecht, 347-354.

McCrea, J.M., 1950, The isotopic chemistry of carbonates and a palaeotemperature scale, J. Chem. Phys. 18, 849-857.

Research Laboratory

File No. 5933

Keith Matthews

Research Laboratory,
The British Museum,
London, WC1B 3DG.

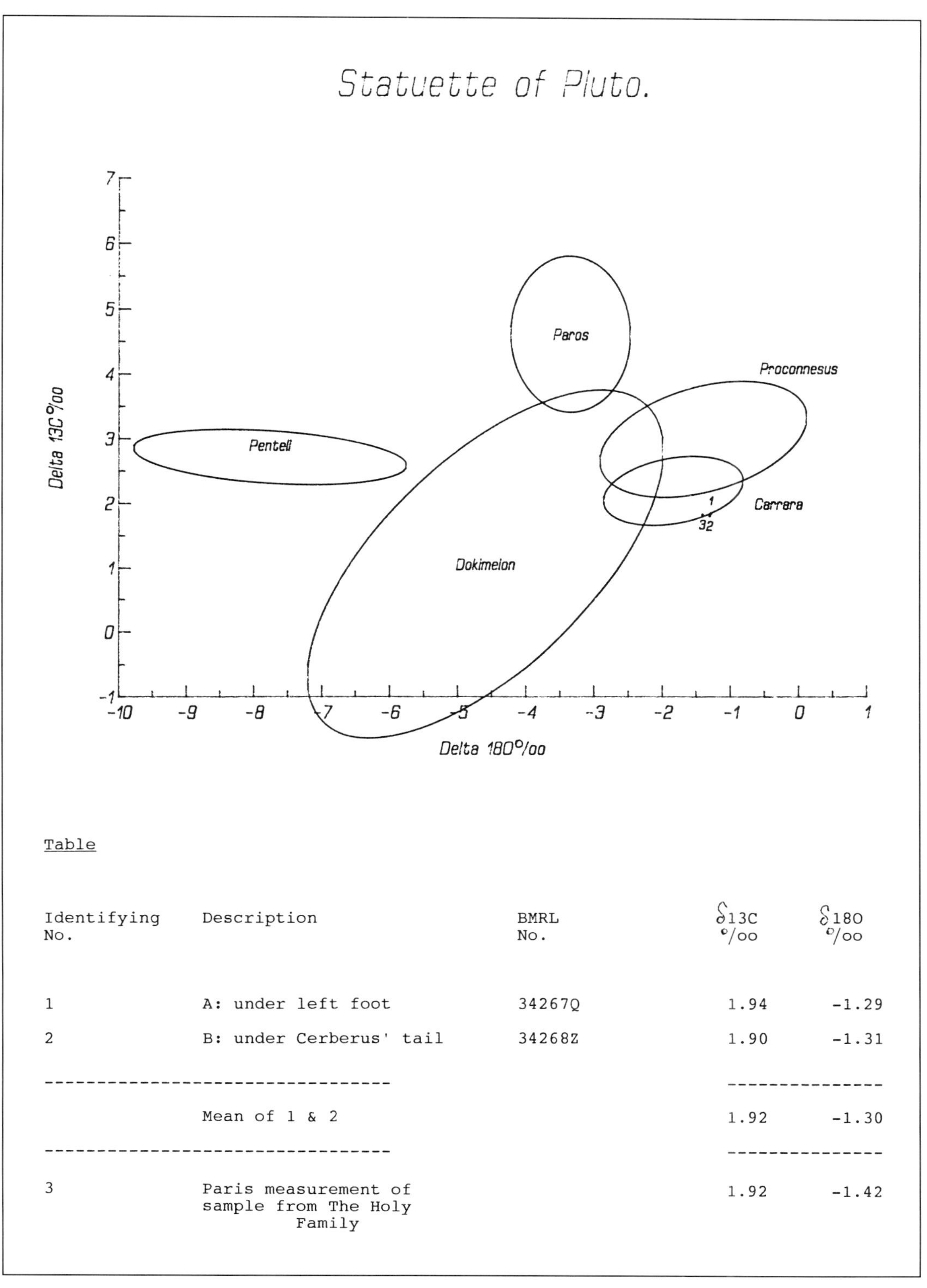

Table

Identifying No.	Description	BMRL No.	δ13C °/oo	δ18O °/oo
1	A: under left foot	34267Q	1.94	-1.29
2	B: under Cerberus' tail	34268Z	1.90	-1.31
	Mean of 1 & 2		1.92	-1.30
3	Paris measurement of sample from The Holy Family		1.92	-1.42

NOTES TO APPENDIX C – numbers 90 to 98

90. Baudry, p. 232. The Carrara white marble quarry was first worked under Julius Caesar and its area extends from near La Spezia on the Mediterranean coast to Lucca inland. Widely exploited for both architecture and sculpture from early times through the Renaissance, its use has been largly limited to sculpture since the beginning of the seventeenth century.

91. op. cit., p. 233. The Saint-Béat white marble quarry is located above the Garonne in the Haute-Pyrénées, up-river from Toulouse. It was opened in Gallo-Roman times and its first working continued into the seventeenth century. It was re-opened in the nineteenth century and has been used since by such sculptors as Pradier, Carpeaux, et al.

92. The actual dimensions for *The Nativity* are: Saint Joseph: h. 1.60 m, w. 1.60 m, d. 0.85 m; The Infant: h. 0.75 m, w. 1.15 m, d. 0.45 m; The Virgin: h. 1.60 m, w. 1.30 m, d. 0.72 m. These measurements have been provided by the Conservation du Service des églises de la Ville de Paris.

93. Baudry, pp. 153 and 581. From Antiquity, through the Middle Ages and the Renaissance, after the extraction at the quarry of the rough block of marble, followed by its cleaning and, often, its squaring-off, the blocking-out stage was frequently accomplished at the site itself to reduce the weight for transporting to the final destination. Beginning with the seventeenth century, however, once the bottom of the block had been stabilised by levelling-out, the usual practice was to send it to the sculptor's workshop for the blocking-out stage.

94. Walker and Matthews, p. 117.

95. Professor Letolle's written communication of 10 January 1990 gives the isotopic analysis for the figure of Saint Joseph as follows:
Delta^{13}C = + 1.92 and Delta^{18}O = − 1.42
('C' for carbon, 'O' for oxygen and + or − figures for fractions of one thousand.)

96. Delta^{13}C = + 2.02 and Delta^{18}O = − 1.84 is the basic isotopic signature for Carrara white marble quarries.
Walker and Matthews explain (p. 117) that the isotopic signature of a quarry is defined by a statistical aggregate of samples.

97. The results of the two isotopic analyses for the figure of *Pluto*, obtained by Mr Matthews (30 January 1990), are as follows:

Description:	Delta^{13}C:	Delta^{18}O:
1 (A) from under left foot	+ 1.94	− 1.29
2 (B) from under Cerberus' tail	+ 1.90	− 1.31

Compare the above with note 95, for Saint Joseph. It will be seen that its carbon reading of + 1.92 falls exactly *between* the two for *Pluto*, indicating an identical marble for the two sculptures. The oxygen variation is insignificant, the difference shown being in fractions of one thousand.

98. There are certain overlaps in the 'data maps' for similar white marbles from quarries in different areas or countries. Consequently, historical, art-historical and visual information must complement an isotopic analysis in identifying the quarry source with certainty (op. cit., p. 117). Professor Letolle, however, has noted in his report that there is a strong probability that the marble of Saint Joseph is from Carrara.

Bibliography

BABELON, Jean-Pierre
'Le Val-de-Grâce redécouvert', *Connaissance des Arts*, no. 446, April 1989, pp. 70–76.

BAUDRY, Marie-Thérèse and BOZO, Dominique
Principes d'analyse scientifique. La Sculpture – Méthode et Vocabulaire, Ministère de la Culture et de la Communication, Paris 1978.

BAZIN, Germain
'Le Val-de-Grâce inconnu', *Connaissance des Arts*, no. 375, May 1983, pp. 98–105.

BENGY-PUYVALLÉE, M. de
Catalogue des Manuscrits de la Bibliothèque de l'Ecole des Beaux-Arts, Paris 1908.

BLUNT, Anthony
'Poussin Studies VI: Poussin's Decoration of the Long Gallery in the Louvre', *The Burlington Magazine*, no. 585, volume XCIII, December 1951, pp. 369–376.

BLUNT, Anthony
Art and Architecture in France 1500–1700, Pelican History of Art, London 1953.

BRESC-BAUTIER, Geneviève, et al
Sculptures des Jardins du Louvre, du Carrousel et des Tuileries, Paris 1986, vol. 2.

BRUEL, A.
'Les Statues et les Bustes du Château de Vaux-le-Vicomte, 1665–1687', *Bulletin de la Société de l'Histoire de Paris et de l'Ile-de-France*, Paris 1880.

CATHEU, Françoise de
'Le Château et le Parc de Sceaux', part I; 'Le Décor du Château et du Parc de Sceaux', part II; *Gazette des Beaux-Arts*, 6e pér., vol. 21, 1939.

CHARAGEAT, Marguerite
Musée du Louvre, *Les sculptures . . . . . . du XVIIe siècle*, Paris 1957, pp. 133–191.

CHARAGEAT, Marguerite
'La Statue d'Amphitrite et la suite des dieux et des déesses de Michel Anguier', *Documents inédits sur l'art français du XVII siècle, Archives de l'art français*, Nouvelle période, vol. xxiii, 1968, pp. 111–123.

DRAPER, James David
'For the Love of Leda', *Metropolitan Museum Bulletin*, November 1971.

DUSSIEUX, L., et al
Mémoires inédits . . ., vol. I, Paris 1854: 'Michel Anguier par Guillet de Saint-Georges, 1690', pp. 435–450.
'Michel Anguier par le Comte de Caylus, 1749', pp. 451–469.

FISCHER, Jacques
editor, *The French Bronze*, Exhibition catalogue, M. Knoedler and Co., New York, 1968.

FRANCASTEL, Pierre
Girardon, Paris 1928.

FRANCASTEL, Pierre
La sculpture de Versailles, Paris 1930.

GONSE, Louis
La Sculpture Française, Paris 1895.

GRIVEL, Marianne
Le Commerce de l'Estampe à Paris au XVIIe Siècle, Paris 1986.

HASKELL, Francis and PENNY, Nicholas
Taste and the Antique: The lure of classical sculpture, New Haven/London 1981.

HEDIN, Thomas
The Sculptures of Gaspar and Balthazar Marsy, University of Missouri, 1983.

HELSDINGEN, H. van
'Anguier over Hercules Farnese', *Nederlands Kunsthistorisches Jaarboek*, vol. 33, 1983.

HOLZHAUSEN, Walter
'Die Bronzen Augusts des Starken in Dresden', *Jahrbuch des Preussischen Kunstsammlungen*, Berlin 1939, vol. 60.

KASSEL, Museum Fridericianum
Aufklärung und Klassizismus, July–October, 1979.

LANDAIS, Hubert
'Some bronzes from the Girardon Collection', *Connoisseur*, 1961, pp. 136–144.

LANDAIS, Hubert
'Mini Monuments', *Art News*, November 1968.

LE COMTE, Florent
Cabinet des Singularités . . ., 3 vols., Paris 1699–1700.

LEEUWENBERG, Jaap and HALSEMA-KUBES, Willy
Beeldhouwkunst in het Rijksmuseum, Amsterdam, 1973.

LESUEUR, Pierre
'La Sculpture de la Porte Saint-Denis à Paris', *Bulletin de la Société de l'Histoire de l'art français*, années 1945–46, Paris 1948, pp. 180–198.

LUGT, Frits
Les Marques de collection de Dessins et d'Estampes, Amsterdam, 1921.

MARIETTE, Pierre-Jean
Abecedario ou notes manuscrites sur les peintres et les graveurs, 10 vols. in fol., Paris 1740–1770. (Microfilms, Cabinet des Estampes, Bibliothèque Nationale, Paris.)

MARIETTE, Pierre-Jean
Abecedario, ed. Ph. de Chennevièvre and A. de Montaiglon, 6 vols., Paris 1851–1860.

MONTAGU, Jennifer
Alessandro Algardi, 2 vols., New Haven/London 1985.

MONTAGU, Jennifer
Roman Baroque Sculpture, New Haven/London 1989.

MONTAIGLON, A. de
Procès-verbaux de l'Académie royale de Peinture et de Sculpture, 1648–1795. 10 vols., Paris, 1875–1892.

MURAT, Inès
Colbert, Paris 1980

NOLHAC, Pierre de
'Les premiers sculpteurs de Versailles', *Gazette des Beaux-Arts*, 3e pér., vol. 21, 1899.

NOLHAC, Pierre de
'Les Bosquets de Versailles', *Gazette des Beaux-Arts*, 3e pér., vol. 22, 1899.

NOLHAC, Pierre de
Les Jardins de Versailles, Paris 1906.

PARIS, Hôtel de la Monnaie
Colbert 1619–1683, October–November 1983, Exhibition catalogue.

RADCLIFFE, Anthony
European Bronze Statuettes, London 1966.

RAGGIO, Olga
'Sculpture in the Grand Manner: Two Groups by Anguier and Monnot', *Apollo*, November 1977, pp. 364–375.

RAGGIO, Olga
'Michel Anguier – *The Flood, 1649*'. In *Notable Acquisitions 1980–1981*, The Metropolitan Museum of Art, New York 1981.

ROBERT-DUMESNIL, A. P. F.
Le Peintre-Graveur Français, 11 vols. Paris 1835–1871.

SAINT-AYMOUR, Caix de
Les Boullongne, Paris 1919.

SANSON, A.
Les Frères Anguier, Rouen 1889.

SOUCHAL, François
'La Collection du sculpteur Girardon d'après son inventaire après décès', *Gazette des Beaux-Arts*, vol. LXXXIII, 1973.

SOUCHAL, François
French Sculptors of the 17th and 18th Centuries – The Reign of Louis XIV, Oxford 1977, 1981, 1987.

STEIN, Henri
Les Frères Anguier, Paris 1889.

THOMASSIN, S.
Recueil des figures, groupes, termes, fontaines, vases et autres ornements tels qu'ils se voyent à présent dans le château et parc de Versailles, Paris 1694.

VILLEMANDI
Catalogue des objets curieux en tous genres de feu M. de Villemandi, Maître André, commissaire-priseur aux ventes, Paris 1788.

WALKER, Dean
The Early Career of François Girardon, 1628–1686: The History of a Sculptor to Louis XIV during the Superintendance of Jean-Baptiste Colbert, New York University, Ph.D. 1982, pub. U.M.I., Ann Arbor, Michigan.

WALKER, Susan and MATTHEWS, Keith
'Recent Work in Stable Isotope Analysis of White Marble in the British Museum', in *Ancient Marble Quarrying and Trade*, Papers from a Colloquium . . ., ed. J. Clayton Fant, Oxford 1988.

WALTON, Guy
Louis XIV's Versailles, Chicago 1986.

WARDROPPER, Ian
'Michel Anguier's Series of Bronze Gods and Goddesses: A Re-examination', *Marsyas*, no. 18, New York 1976.

WASHINGTON, National Gallery of Art, et al.
The Splendor of Dresden, June 1978–May 1979; particularly: 'The Collection of Bronzes', introduction and entries by Martin Raumschüssel.

WEIGERT, Roger-Armand
Inventaire du Fonds Français – Graveurs du XVIIe Siècle, 7 vols., Paris 1939–1976.

WEIGERT, Roger-Armand
'Les deux premiers Mariette et François Langlois', *Gazette des Beaux-Arts*, vol. 41, March 1953.

WEIGERT, Roger-Armand
La gravure et la renommée de Poussin (Colloque sur Nicolas Poussin), Editions du C.N.R.S., Paris 1958, pp. 277–283.

WEIHRAUCH, H. R.
Die Europäische Bronzestatuetten, Braunschweig 1967.

WIRENIUS-MAZULEVITCH, Mme
'Les bronzes français du XVIIe au Musée de l'Ermitage', *Gazette des Beaux-Arts*, June 1925, p. 332.

Plates

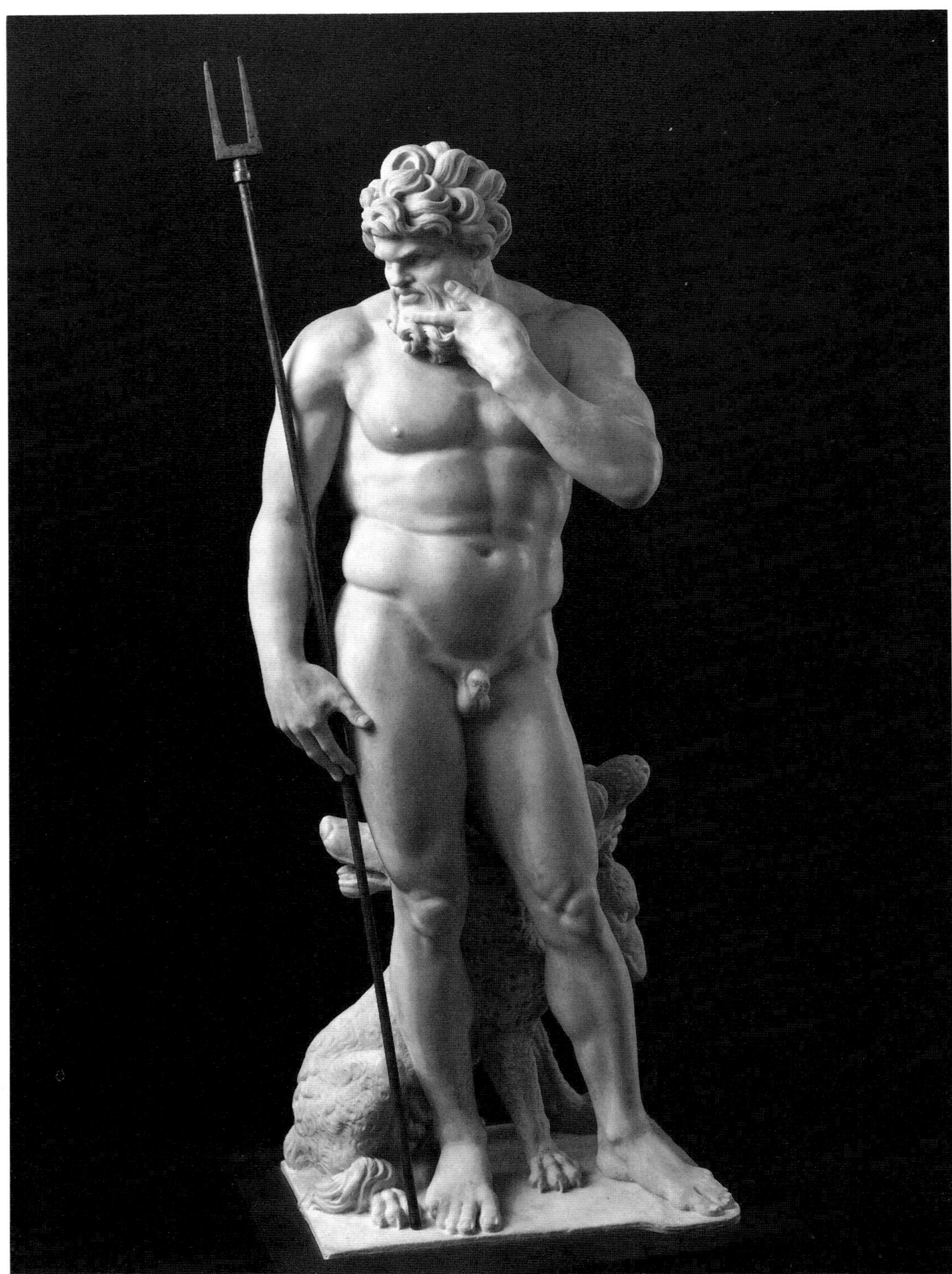

Plate 1
Michel Anguier, *Pluto*, marble, before 1669, height: 73 cm.
Private collection.
'This god Pluto here should be of short and strong proportions . . .'.
– Michel Anguier, in his lecture of 1676.

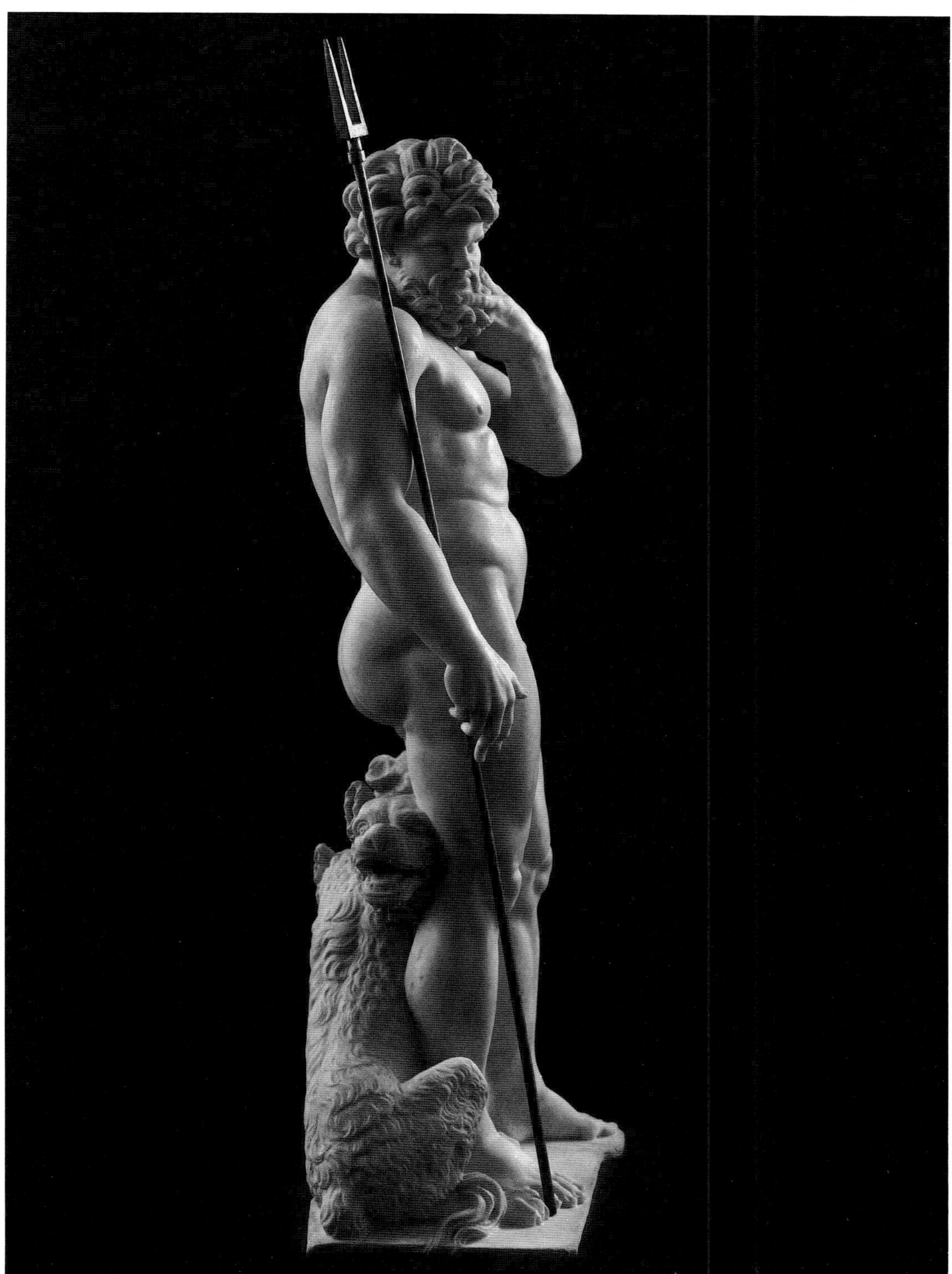

Plate 2
Right-hand view of Plate 1.
'. . . his flesh heavy . . . his muscles plump and sagging . . .'.
– Michel Anguier, in his lecture of 1676.

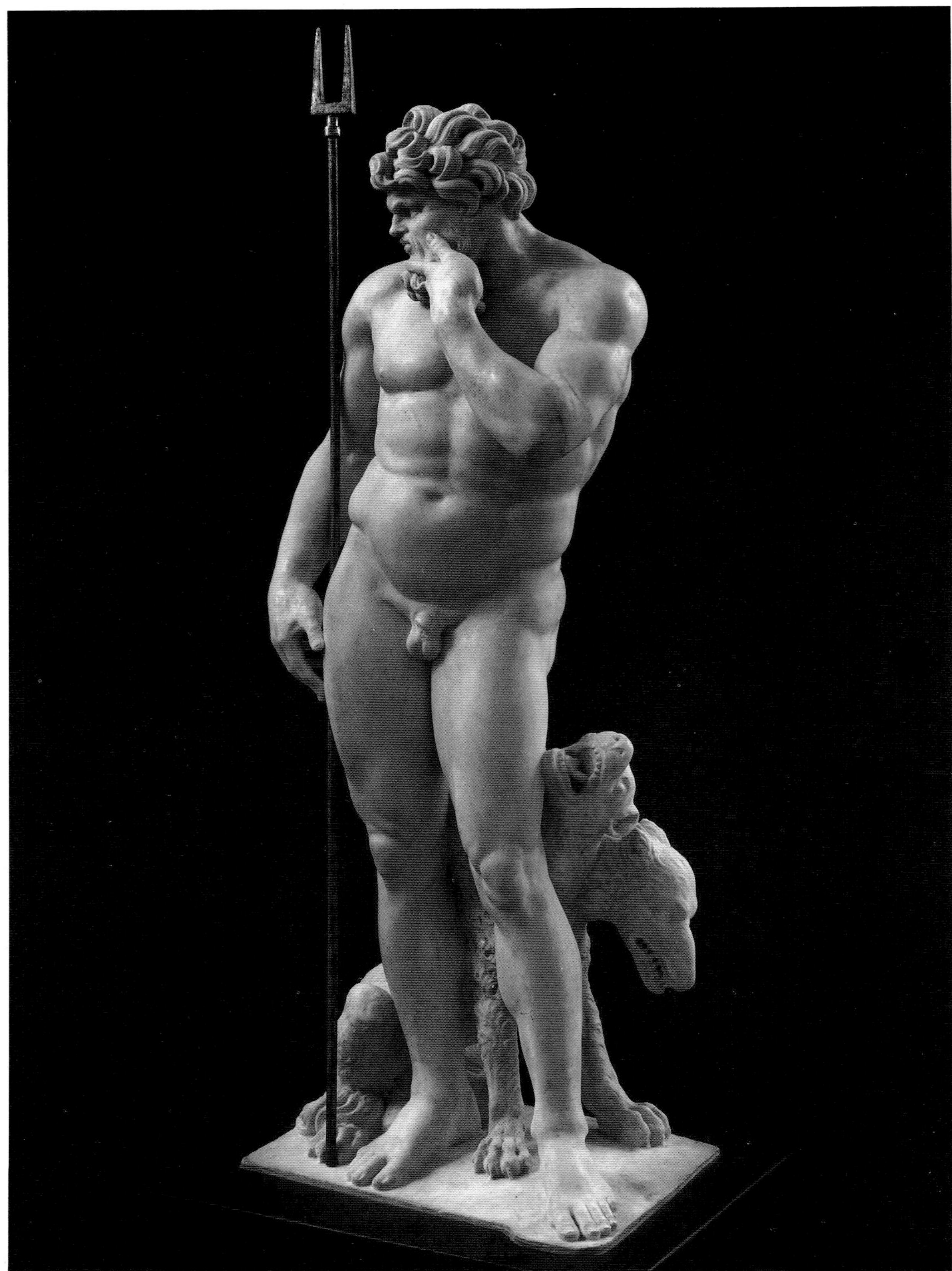

Plate 3
Three-quarter view of Plate 1.
'. . . this figure of *Pluto* that I have represented in a cold and arid melancholy . . .'.
– Michel Anguier, in his lecture of 1669.

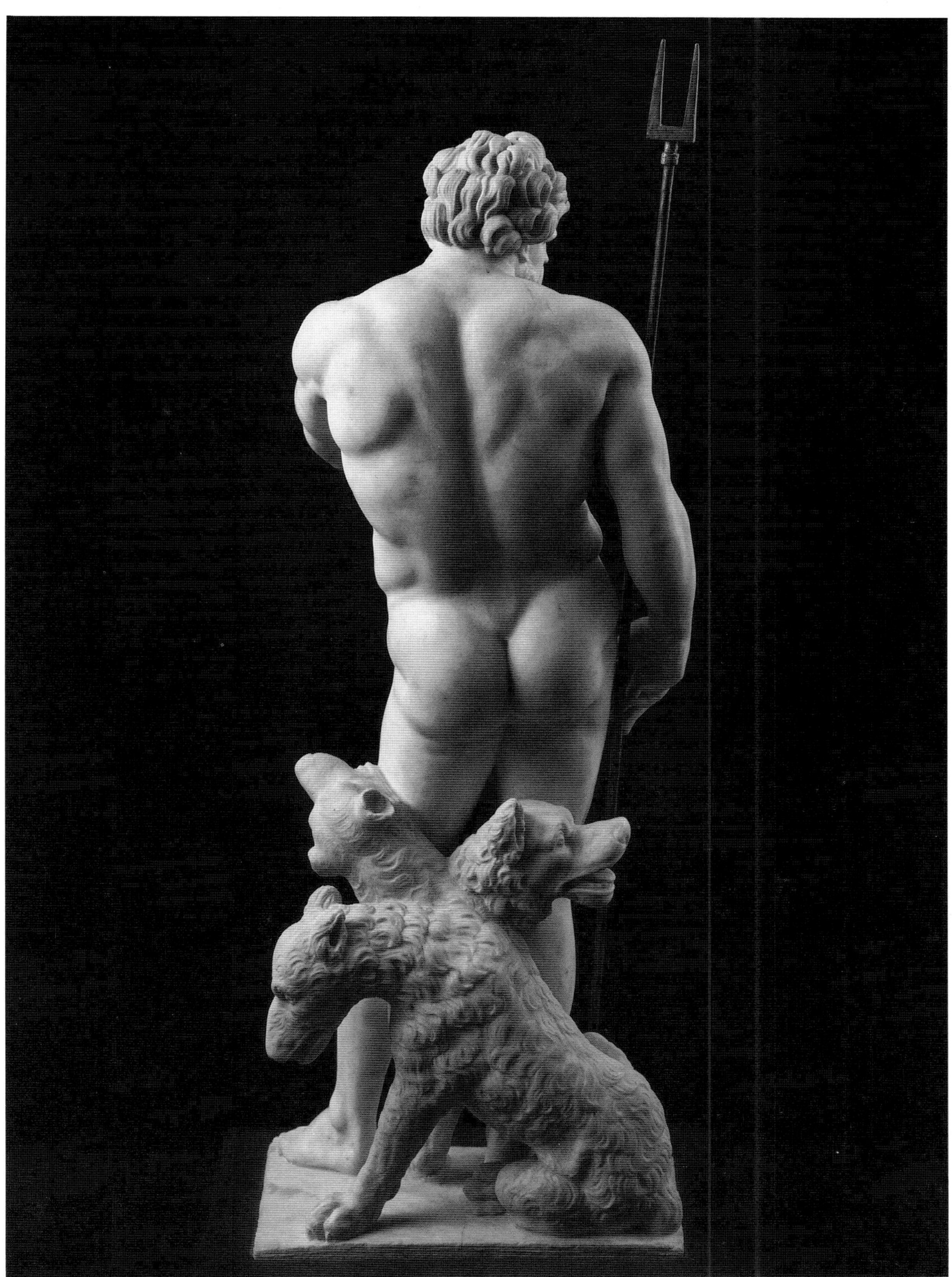

PLATE 4
Rear view of PLATE 1.
Compare treatment of ear on left-hand head with the lambs's ear in PLATE 33.

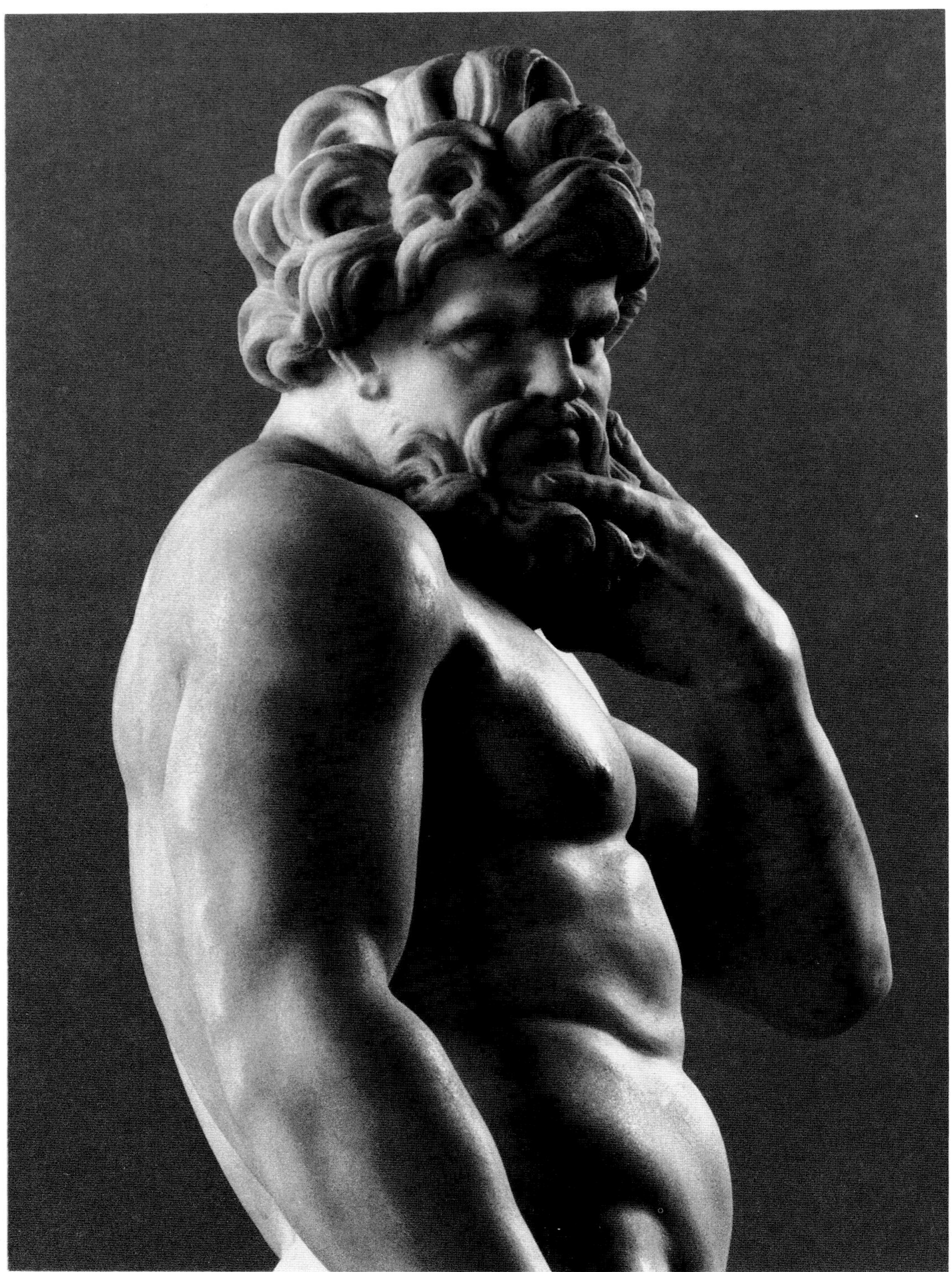

Plate 5
Detail of Plate 1.
'. . . the expression on his face indicating melancholy . . . '.
– Michel Anguier, in his lecture of 1676.

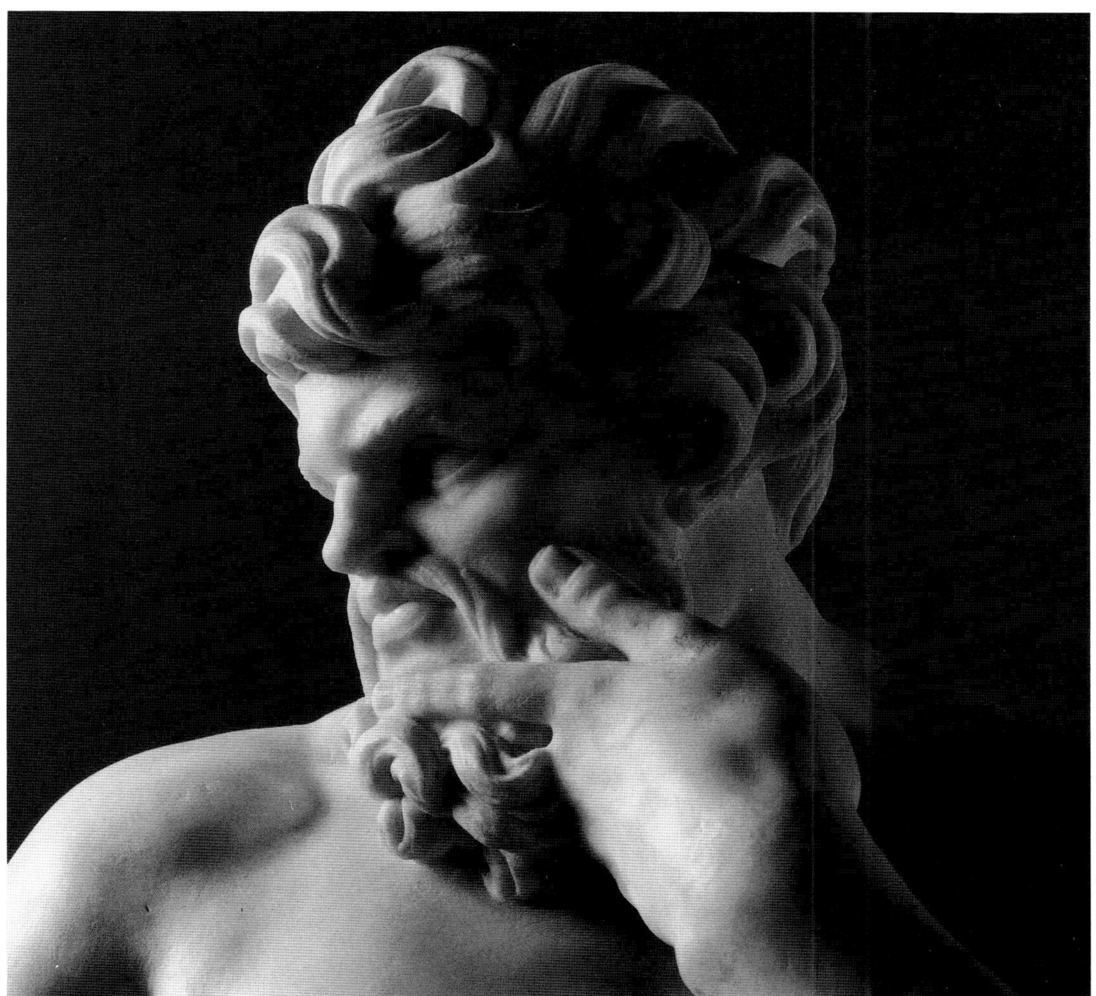

PLATE 6
Detail of PLATE 1.
Compare hand with PLATES 28 and 30.

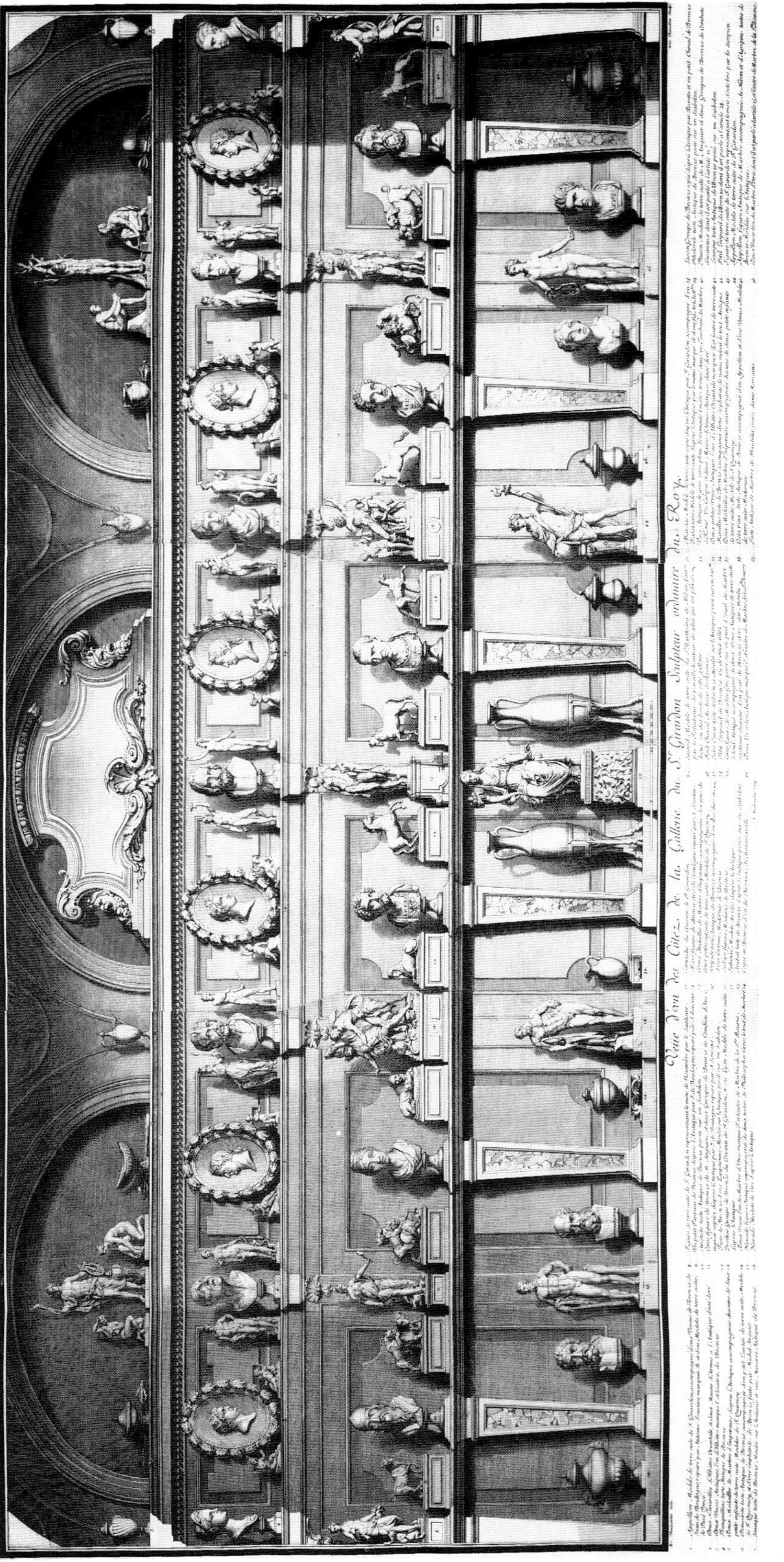

Plate 7
Chevallier, after a drawing by Charpentier, '*Galerie de Girardon*',
plate III, engraving, circa 1710.
London, B.M., Dept. Prints

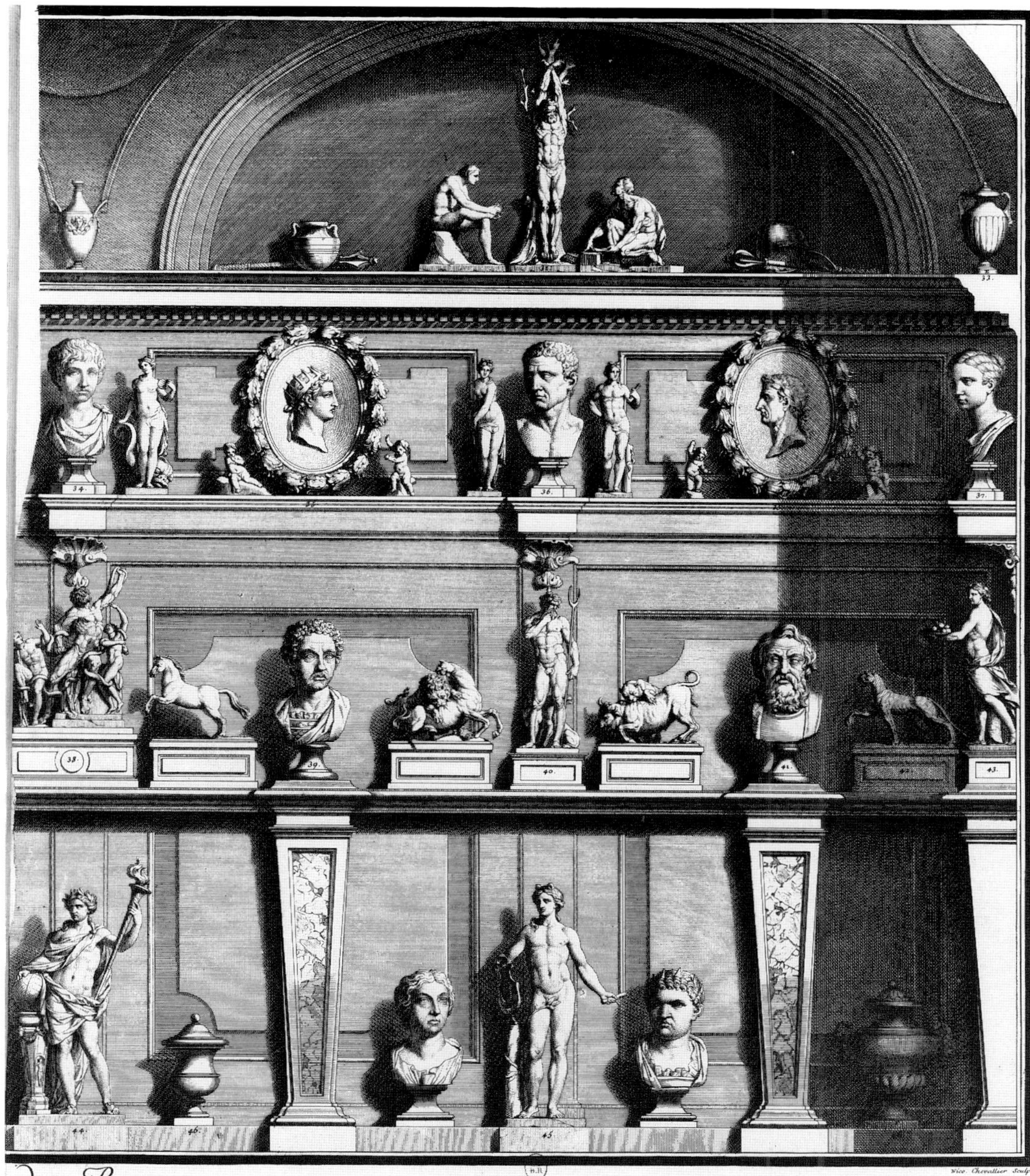

PLATE 8

Detail of PLATE 7, showing the terracotta model of *Pluto*.
In the engraved legend, no. 40 is described as:
'*Pluton Modèle de terre cuite de M. Anguier . . .*'.
Paris, B.N., Cabinet des Estampes.

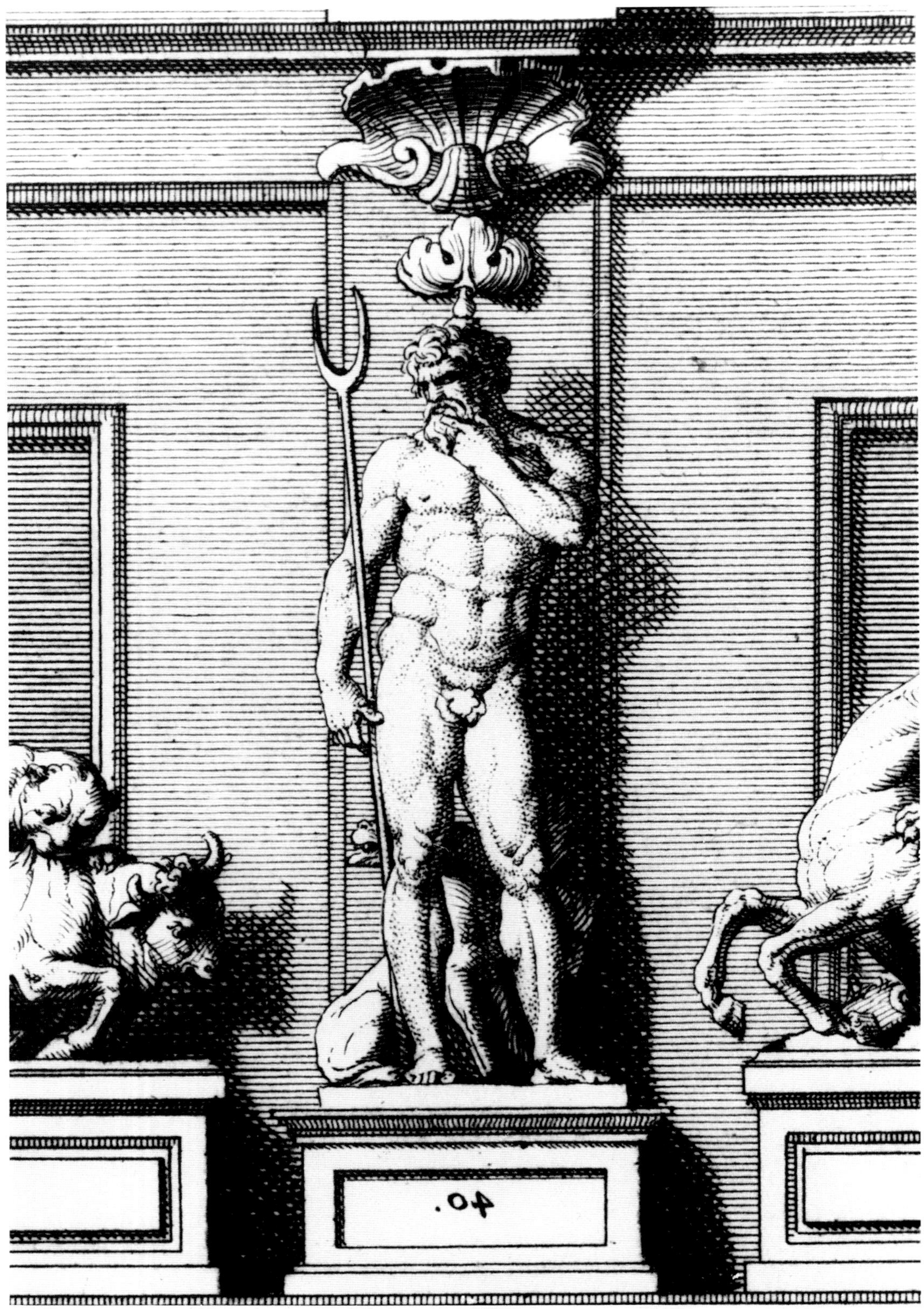

Plate 9
Detail of Plate 7, printed in reverse for comparison.

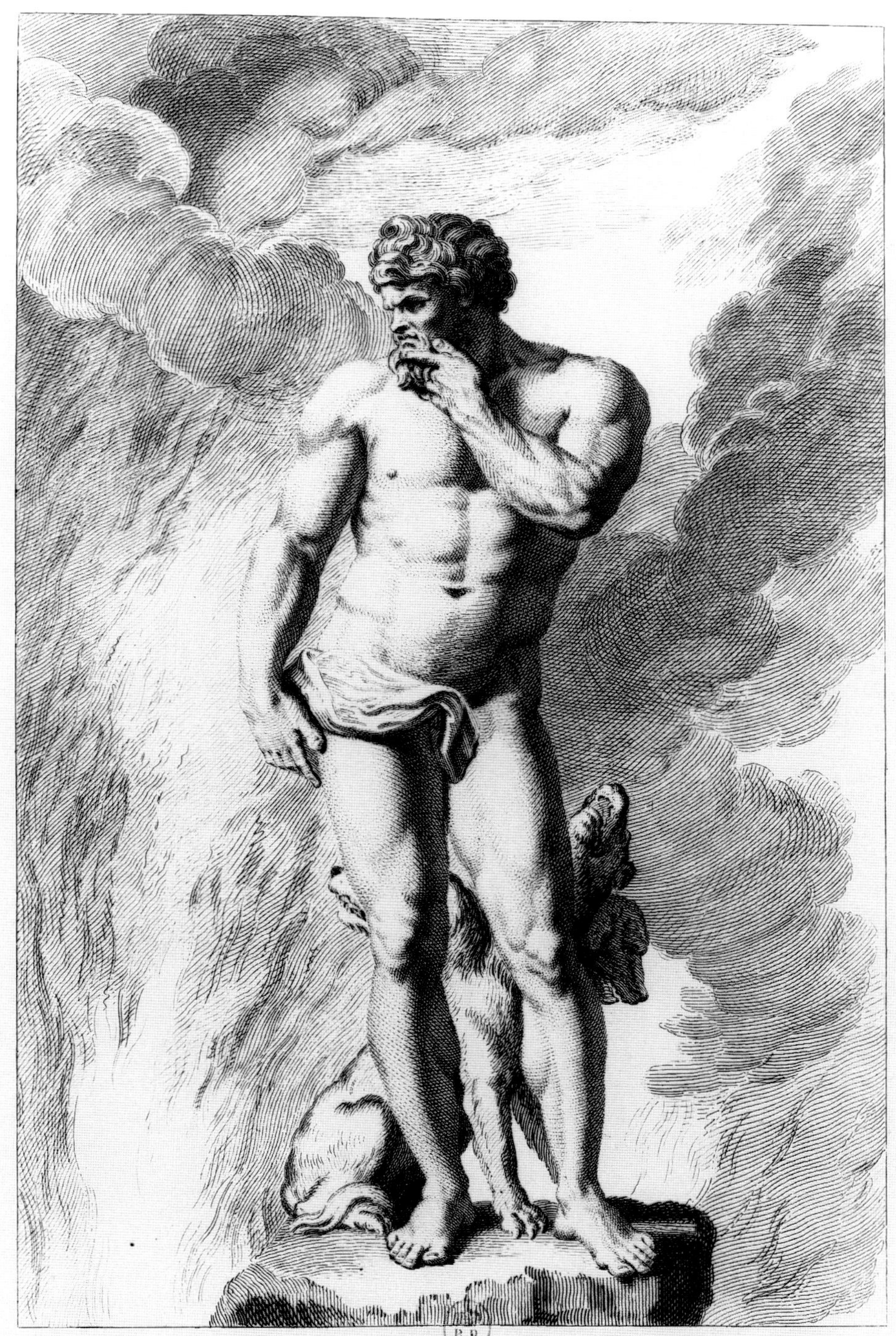

Plate 10
Louis Desplaces, *Pluto*, after Michel Anguier, engraving, early eighteenth century.
Paris, B.N., Estampes.

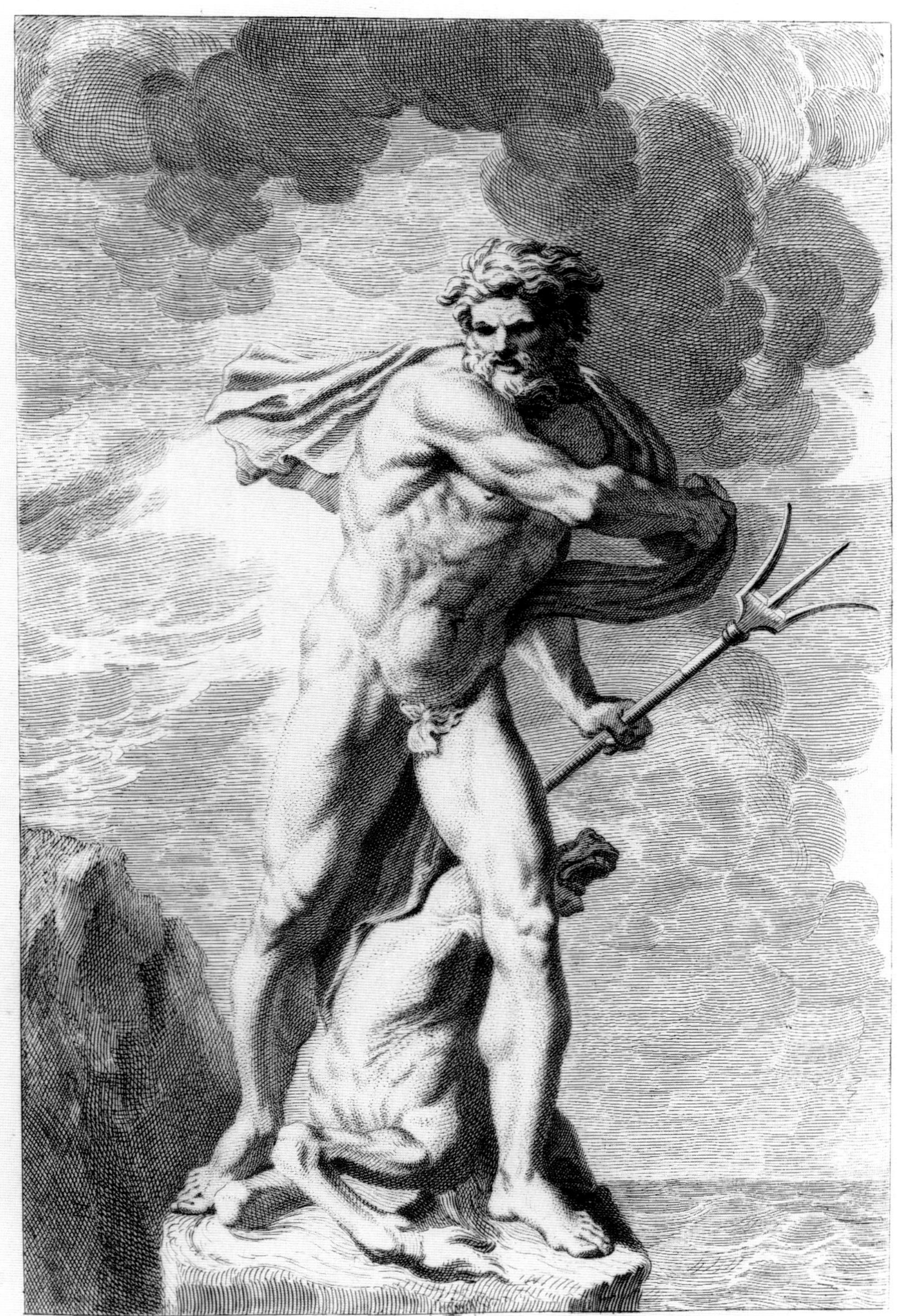

PLATE 11
Louis Desplaces, *Neptune*, after Michel Anguier, engraving, early eighteenth century.
Paris, B.N., Estampes.

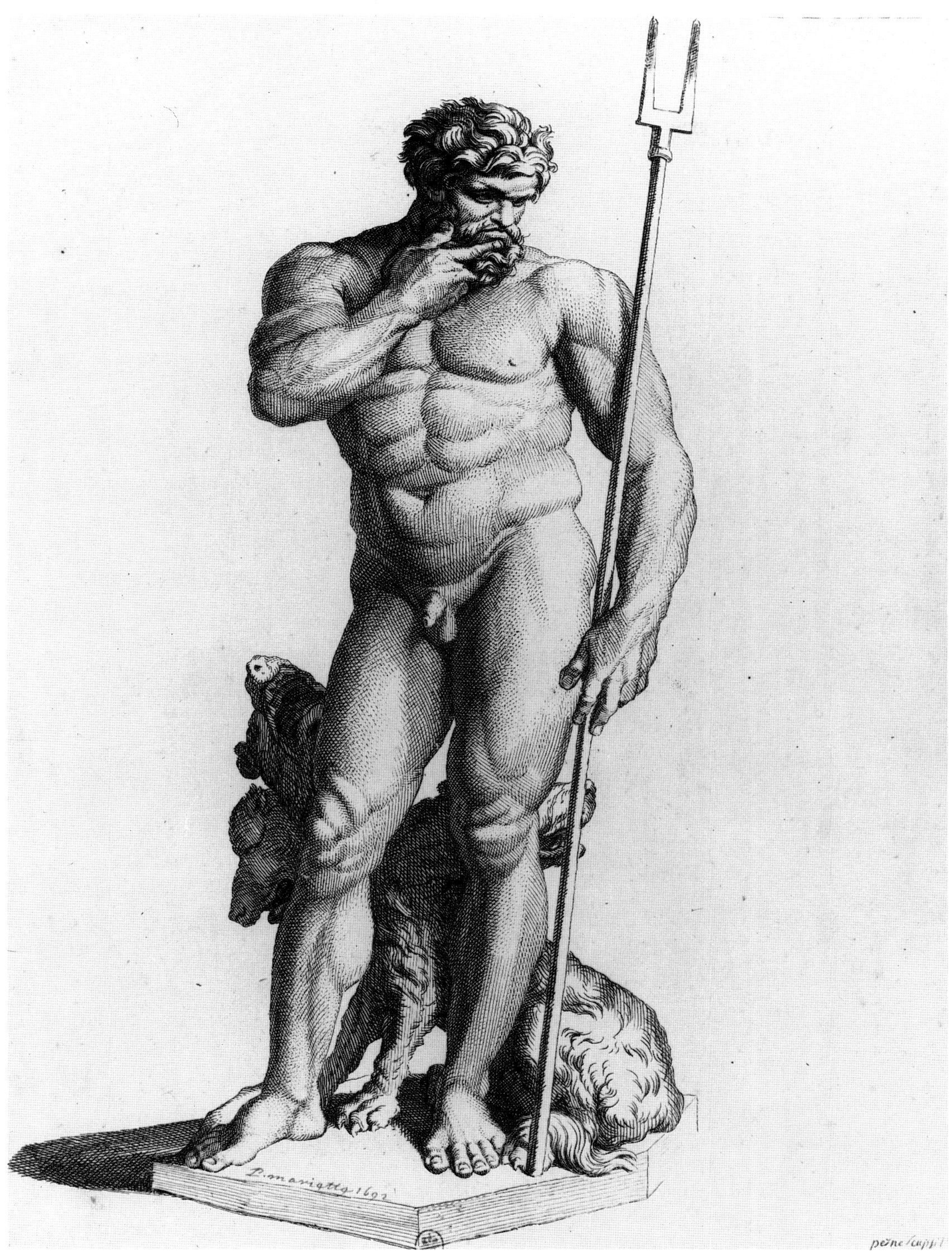

PLATE 12
Jean Pesne, *Pluto*, after Michel Anguier, engraving,
first 'nude' state, with added signature and date: 'P. Mariette 1692'.
Paris, B.N., Estampes.
The viewpoint, looking down, is indicative of the
figure's small scale. Compare with PLATE 18.

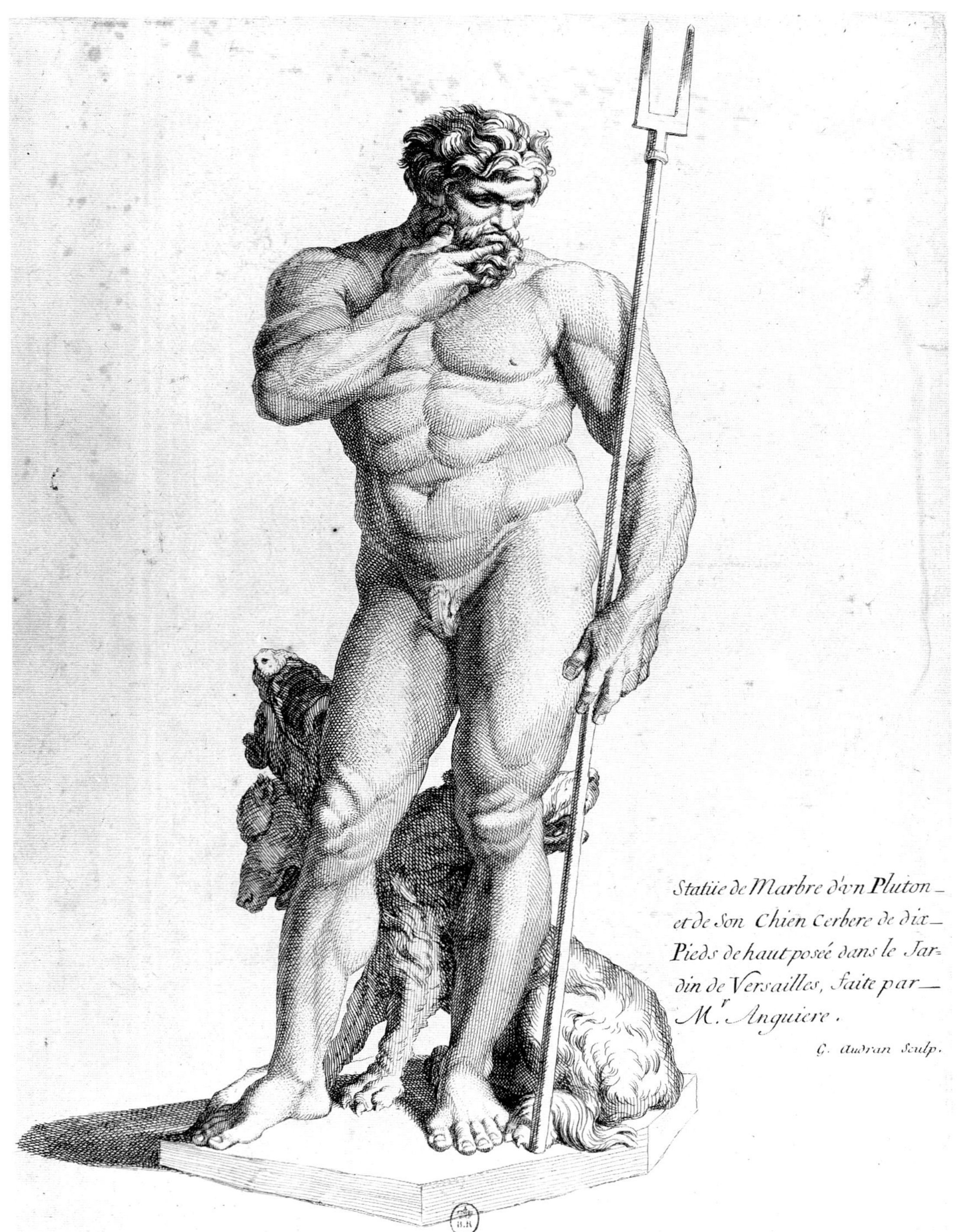

PLATE 13
Jean Pesne, *Pluto*, after Michel Anguier, engraving, second 'fig-leaf' state with later, erroneous inscription ascribing it to Gérard Audran.
Paris, B.N., Estampes.

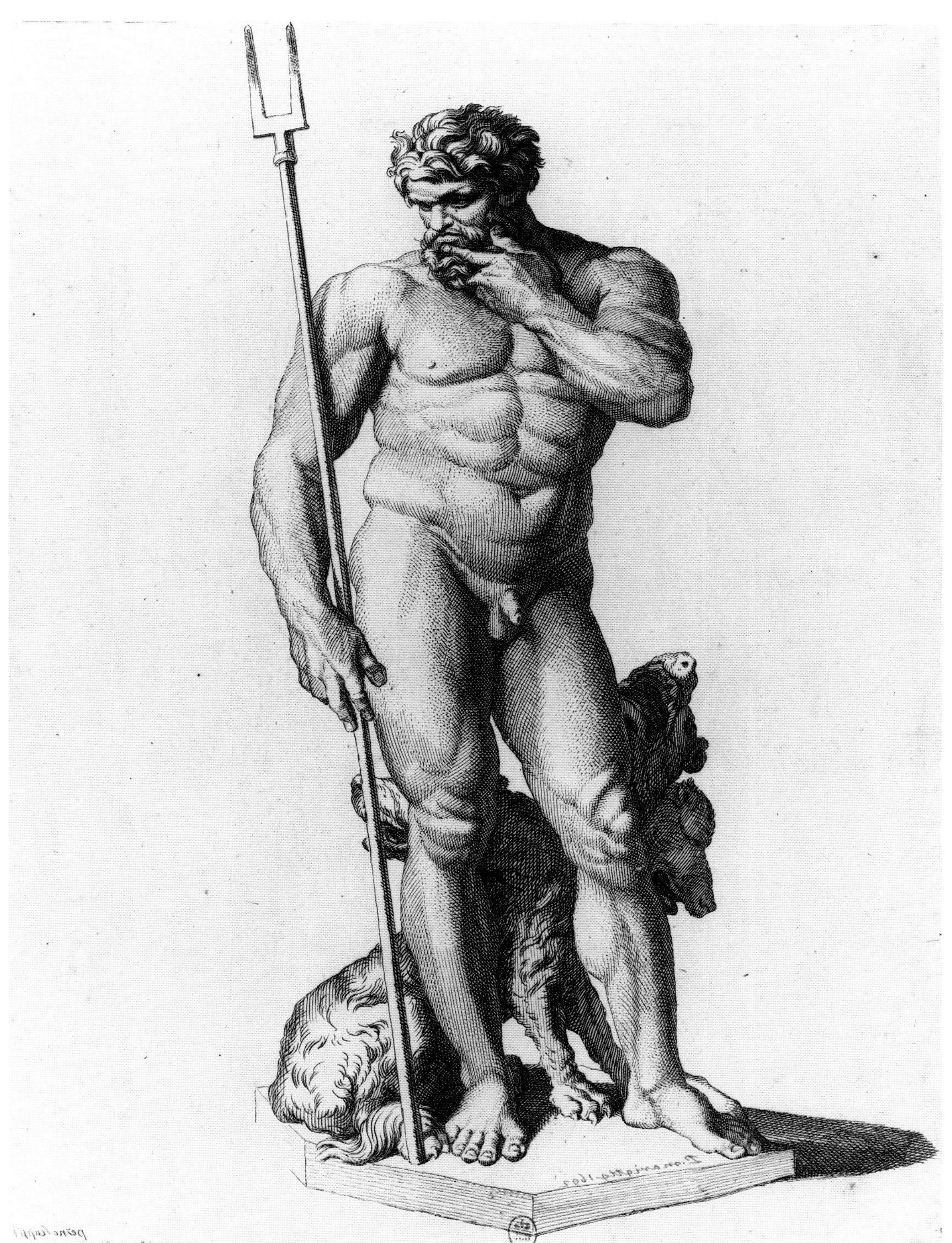

Plate 14
Plate 12, printed in reverse. Compare with Plate 1.
Paris, B.N., Estampes.

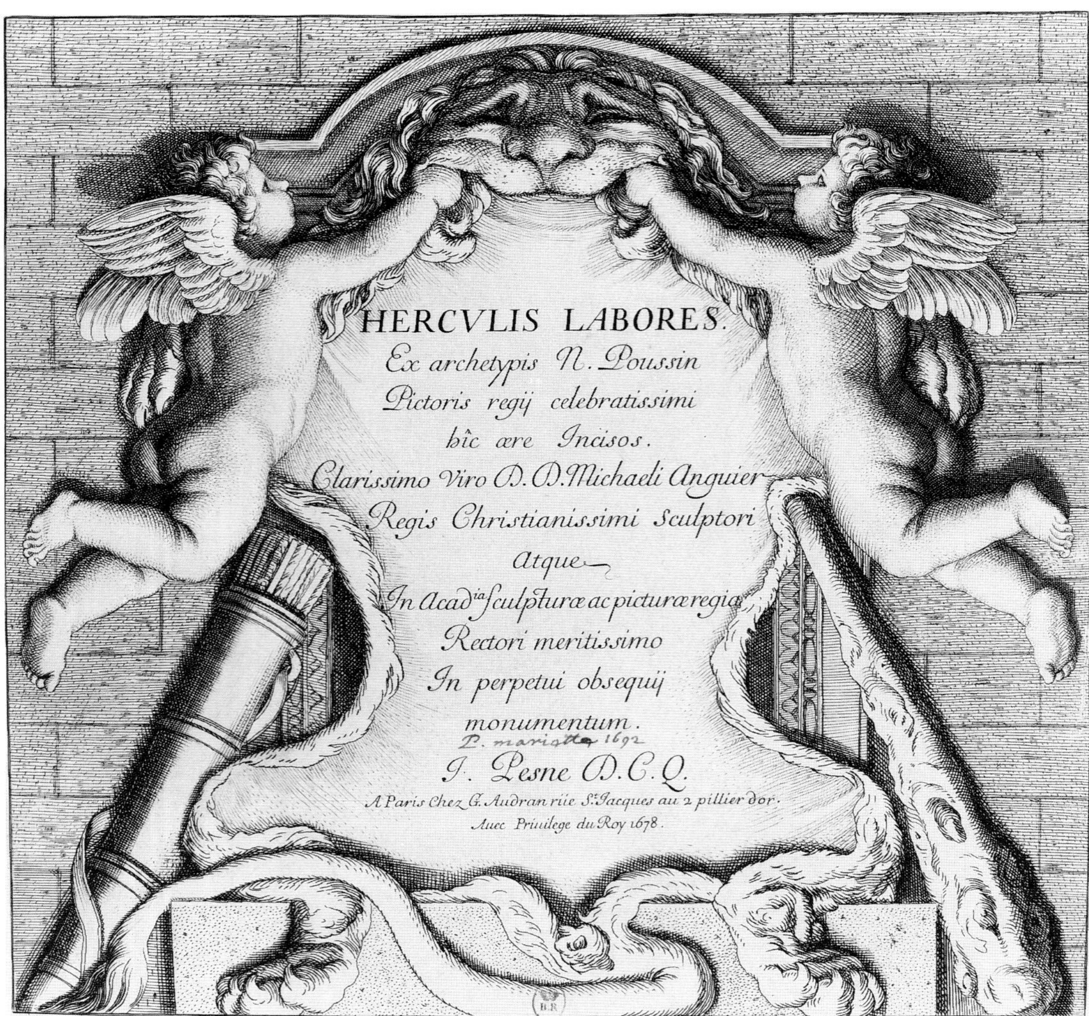

Plate 15
Jean Pesne, *Les Travaux d'Hercule*, frontispiece with dated dedication to Michel Anguier, engraving, 1678.
Also with added signature and date: 'P. Mariette 1692'.
Paris, B.N., Estampes.

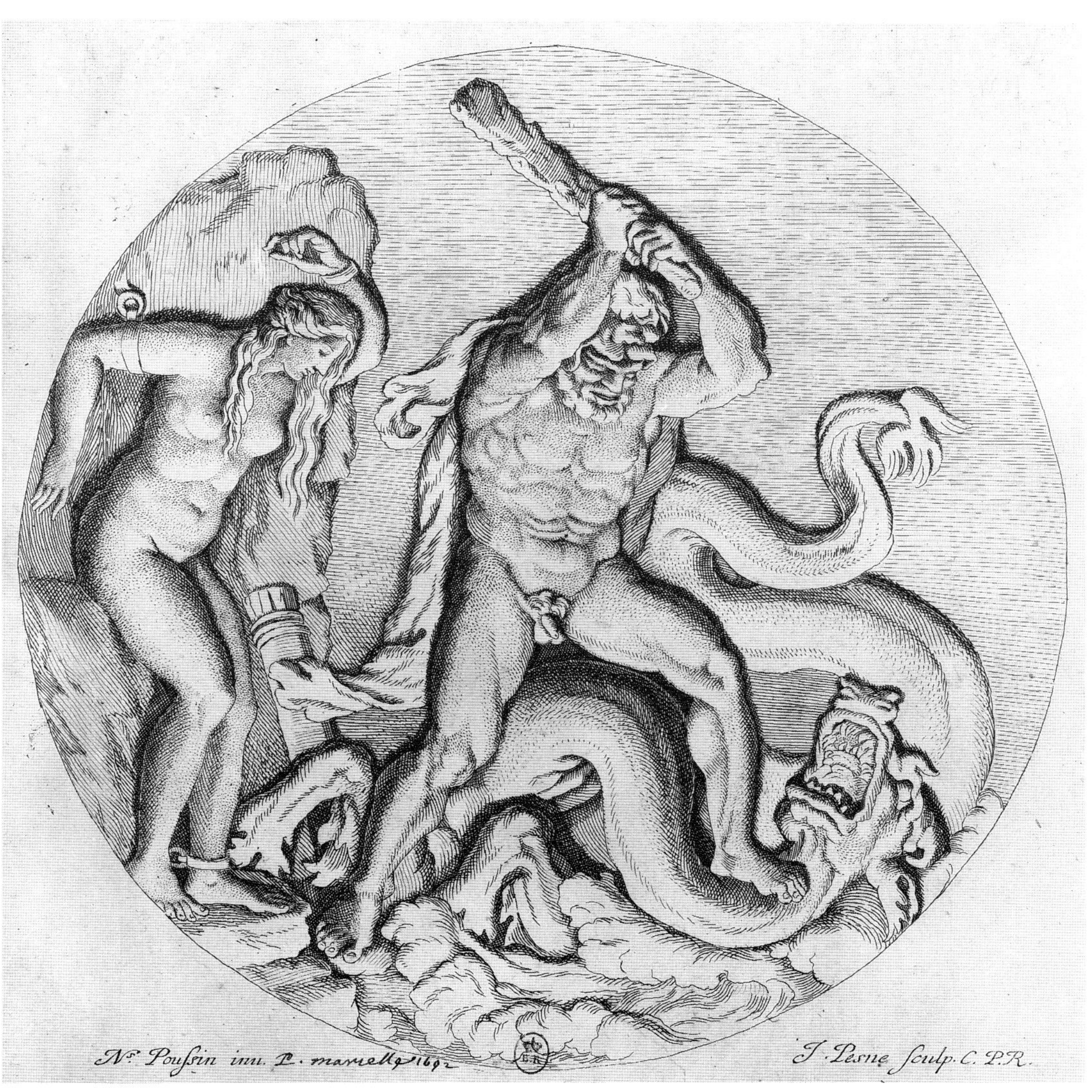

Plate 16
Jean Pesne, a plate from *Les Travaux d'Hercule*, engraving, after Poussin, 1678. Also with 'Mariette' signature and date. Paris, B.N., Estampes.

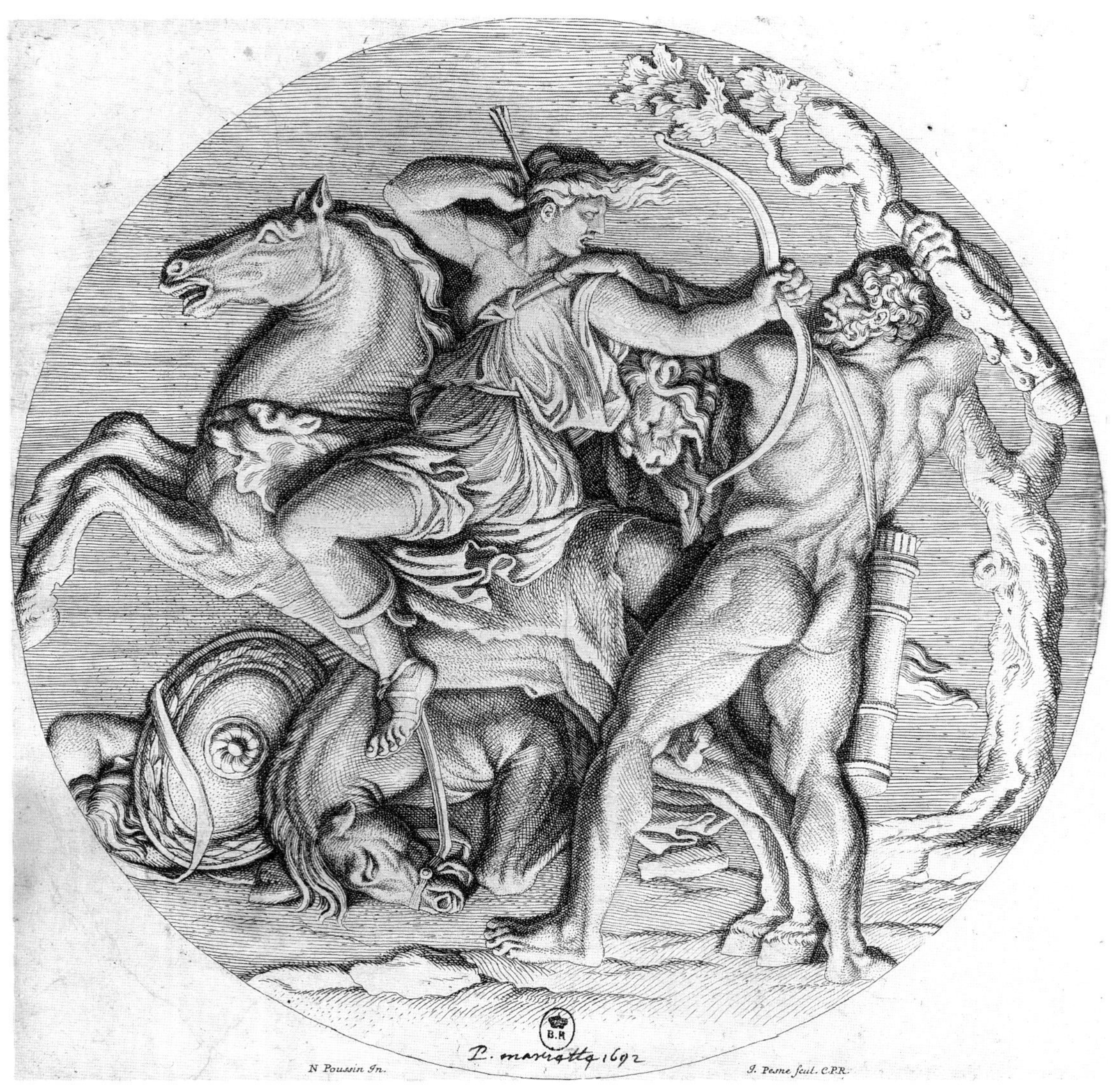

Plate 17
Jean Pesne, another plate from *Les Travaux d'Hercule*, engraving after Poussin, 1678. Also with 'Mariette' signature and date. Paris, B.N., Estampes.

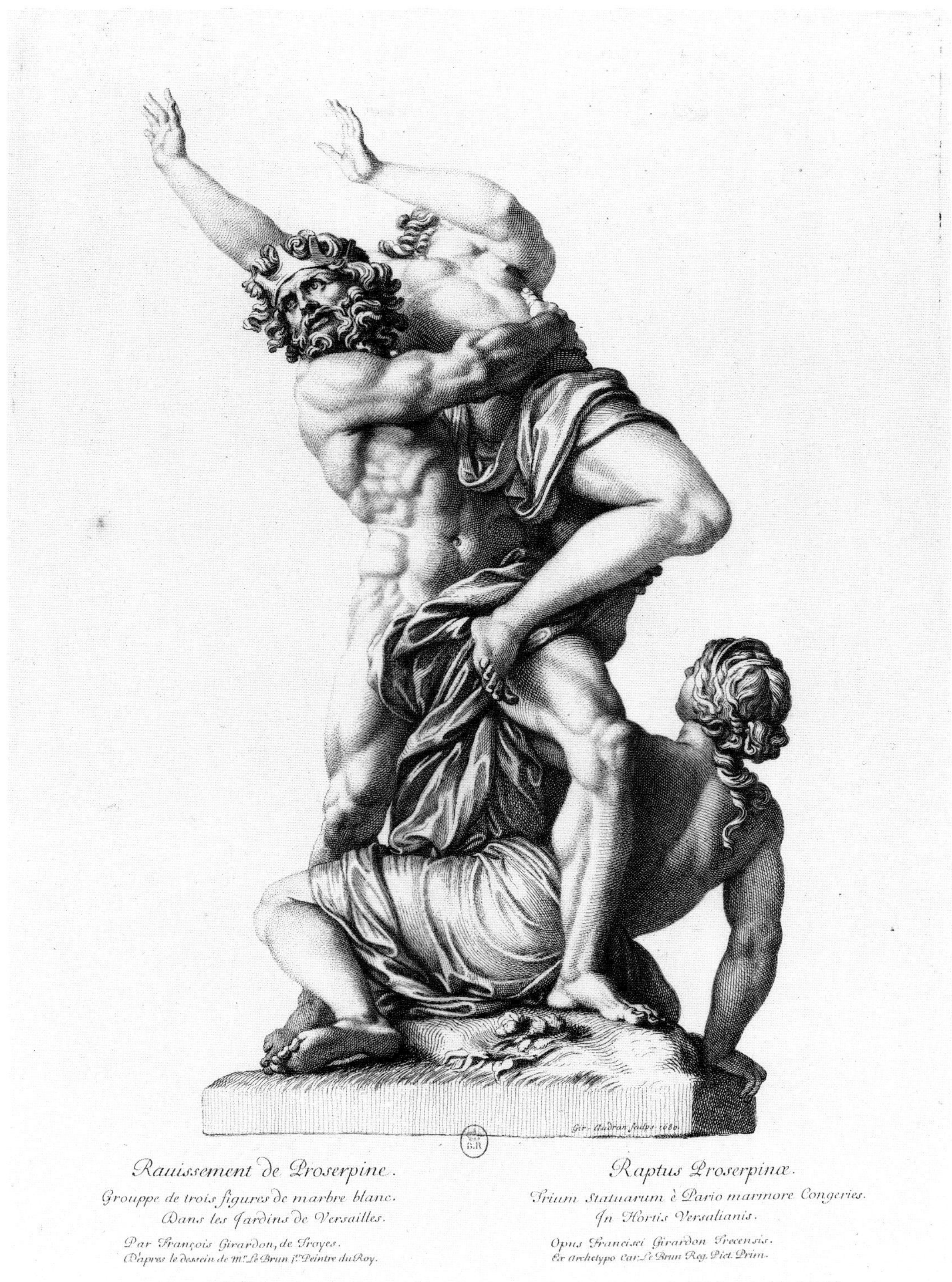

PLATE 18
Gérard Audran, *The Rape of Proserpine*, engraving after Girardon, 1680. Note the viewpoint from below. Paris, B.N., Estampes.

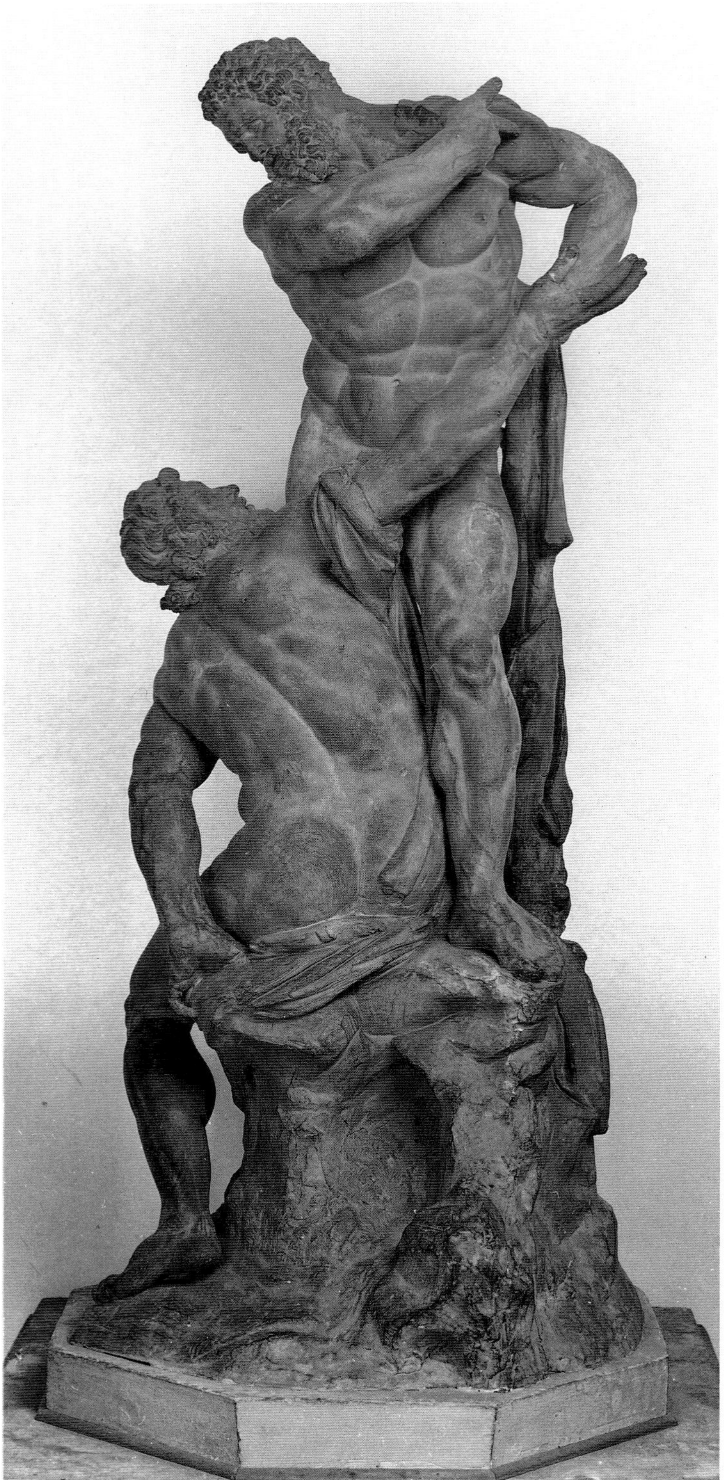

Plate 19
Michel Anguier, *Hercules and Atlas*, terracotta, before 1669, height: 130cm. The octagonal wood base is later.
Paris, Louvre.

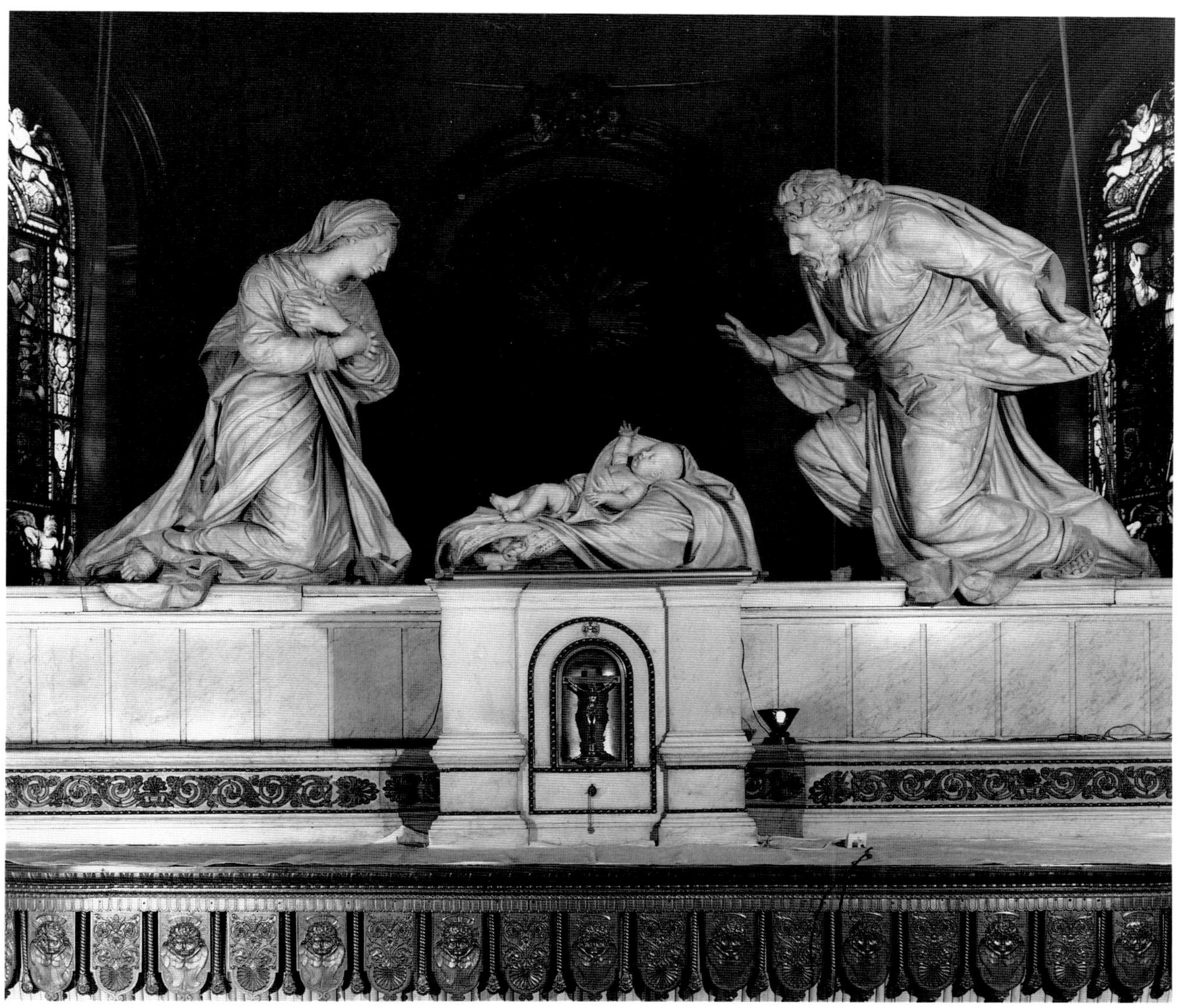

Plate 20
Michel Anguier, *The Nativity*, marble, 1665–1667.
Paris, Eglise Saint-Roch.
Germain Bazin of the Institut de France has described this group (1983) as 'a masterpiece of the world's sculpture'.

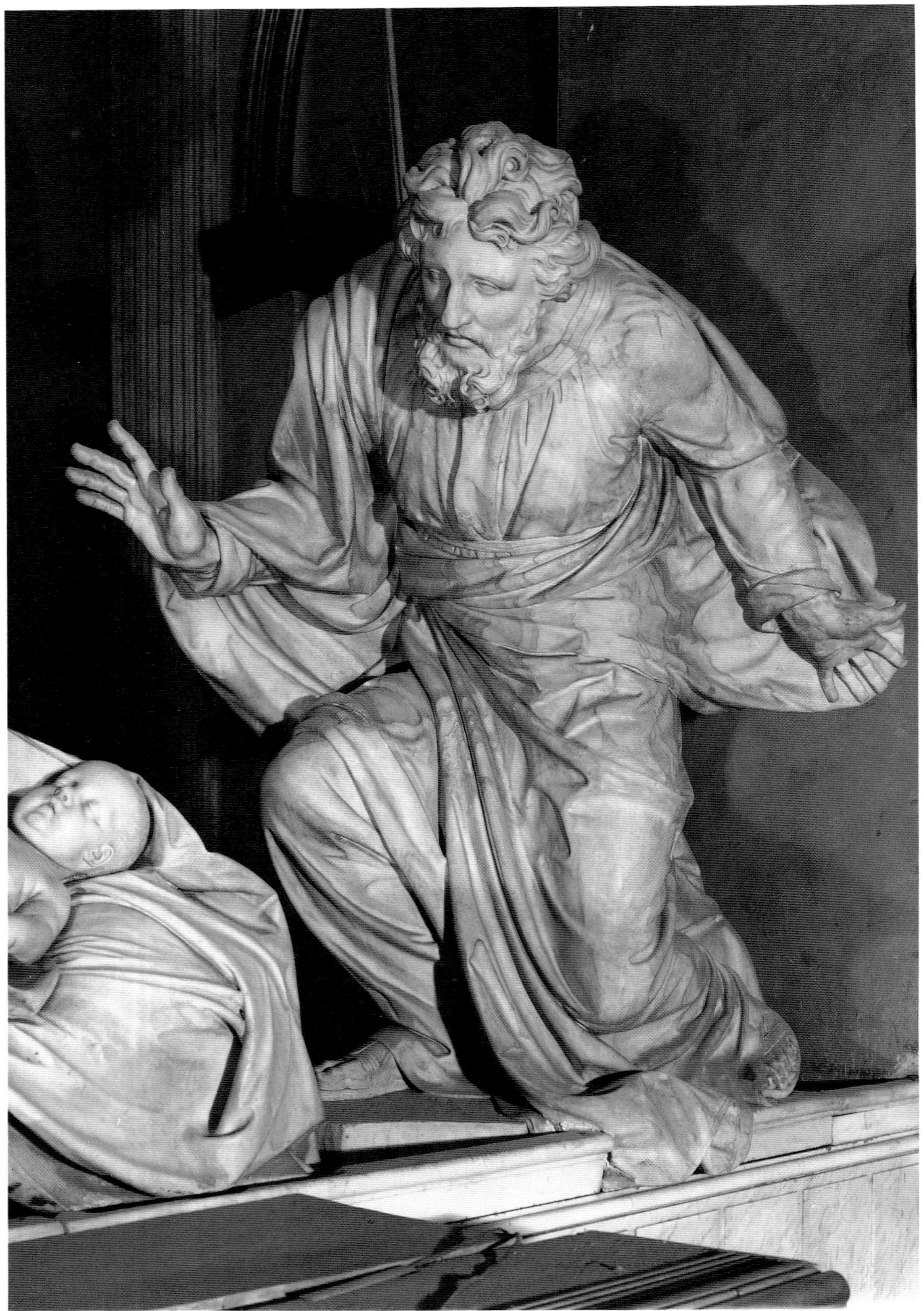

Plate 21
Detail of Plate 20: Saint Joseph.

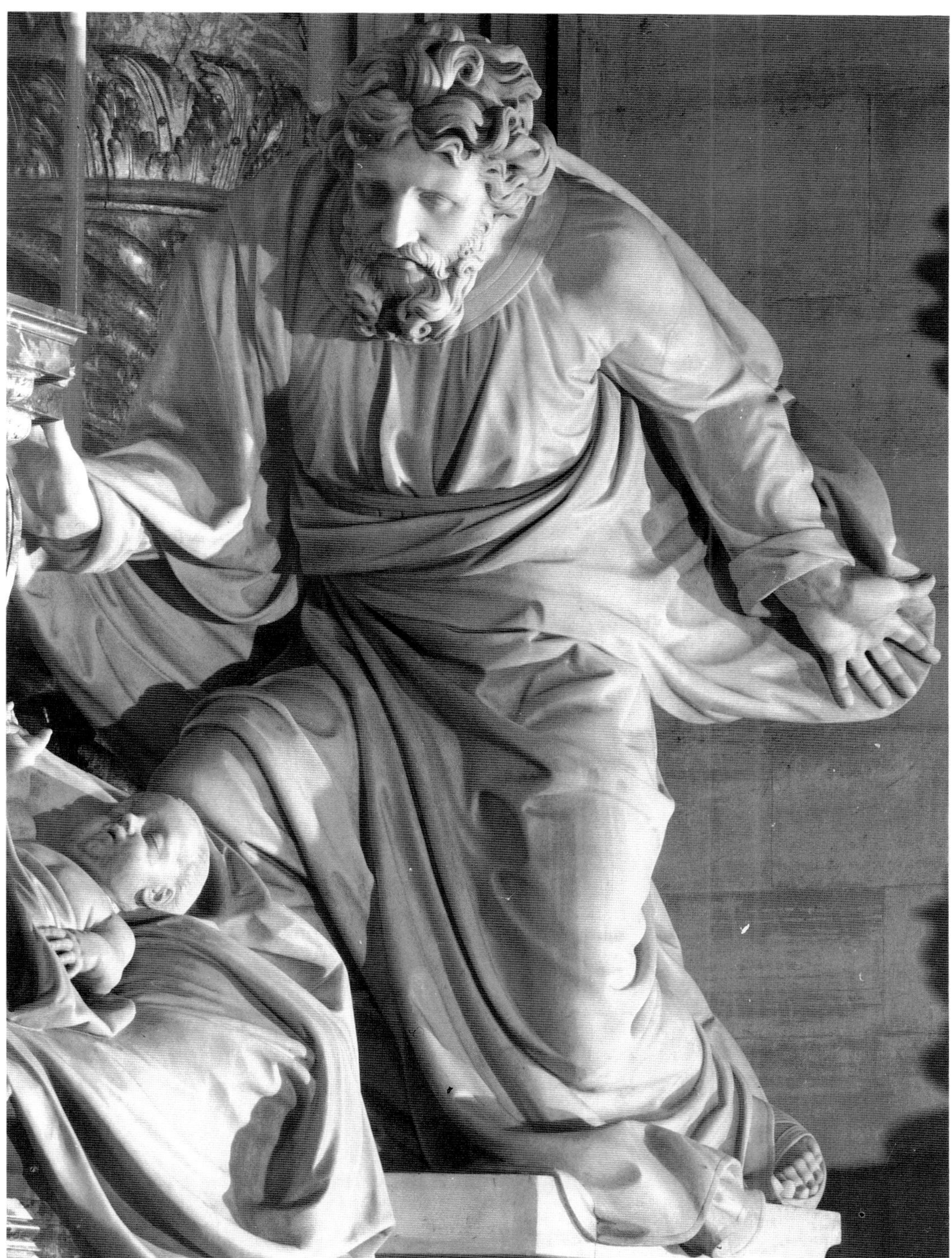

Plate 22
Louis-Antoine Desprey, Saint Joseph in *The Nativity*, after Michel Anguier, marble, 1869.
Paris, Val-de-Grâce.

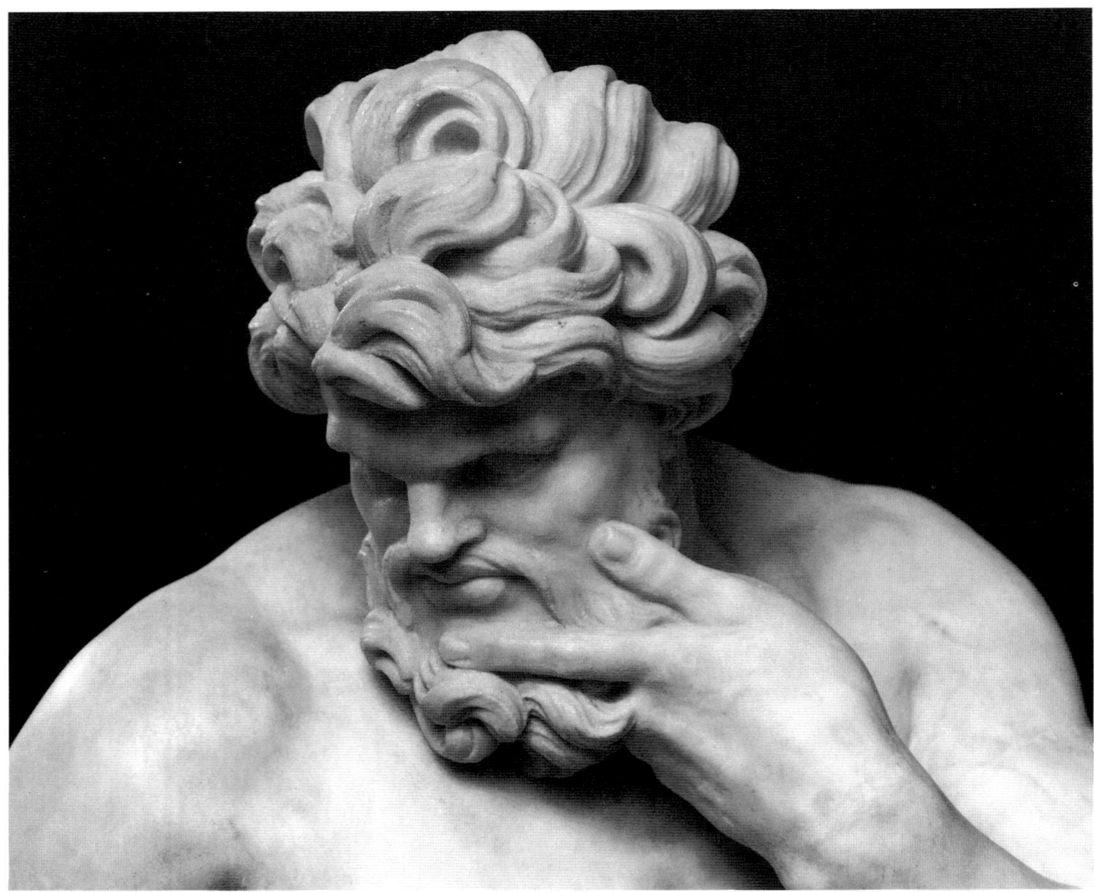

Plate 23
Detail of Plate 1. Notice the deep undercutting of the locks of hair.

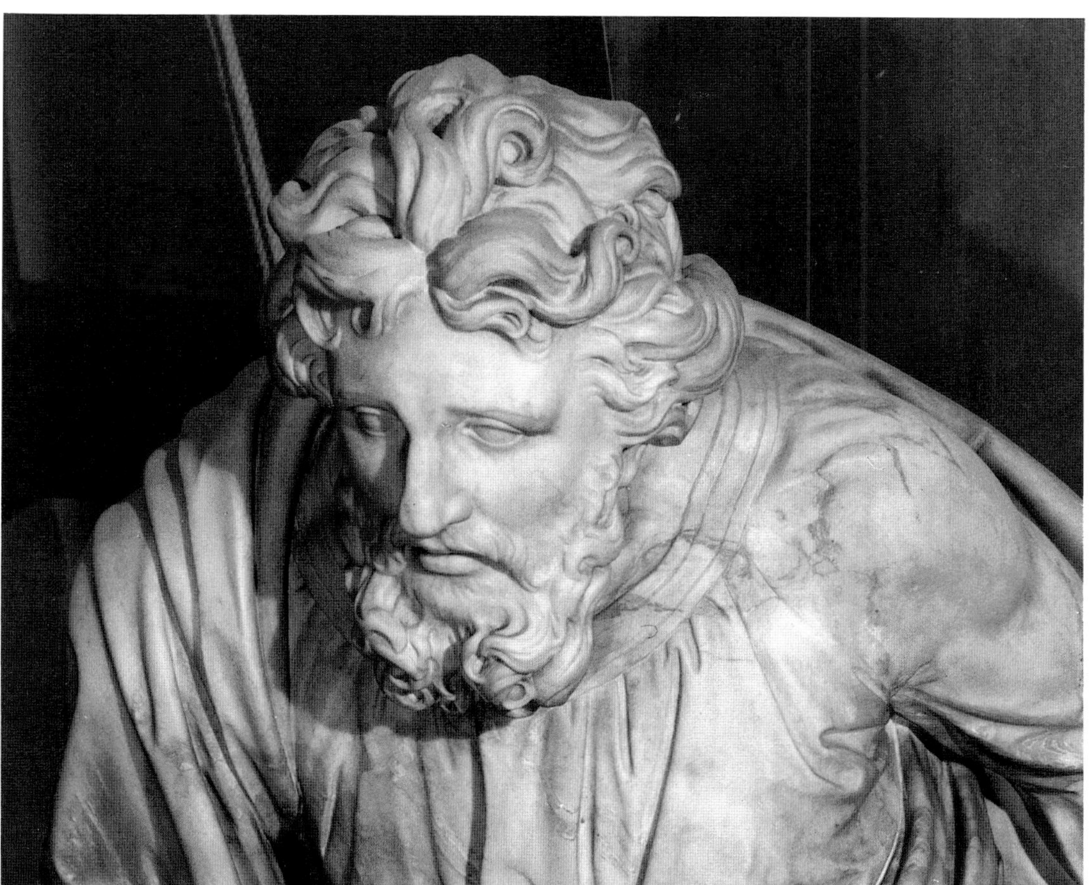

PLATE 24
Enlarged detail of PLATE 21. Compare carving of hair with that of *Pluto*, PLATE 23.

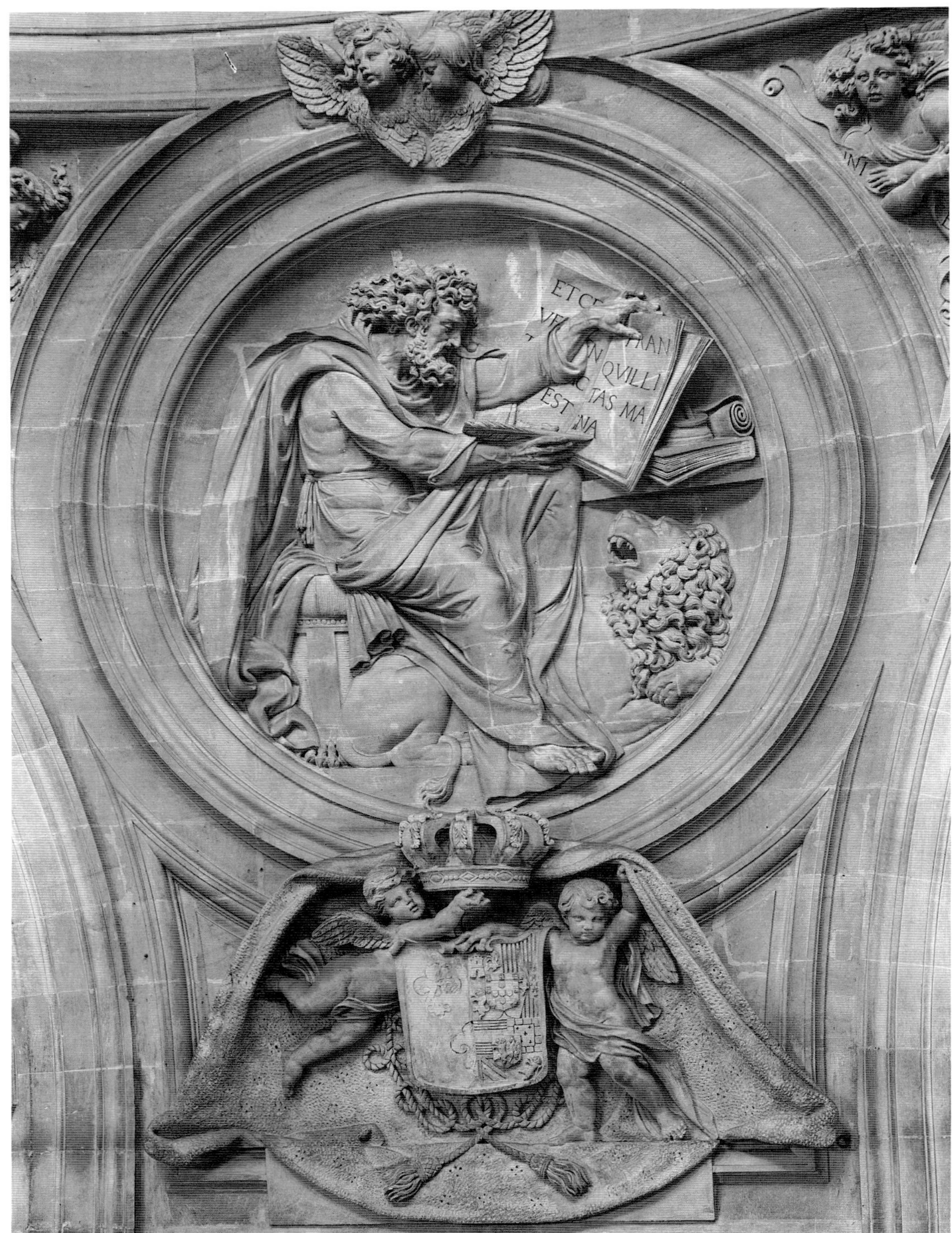

PLATE 25
Michel Anguier, *Saint Mark*, stone relief, partly in the round, diameter 3.5 metres. One of the four Evangelists decorating the spandrels under the dome of the church; executed between 1662 and 1667.
Paris, Val-de-Grâce.

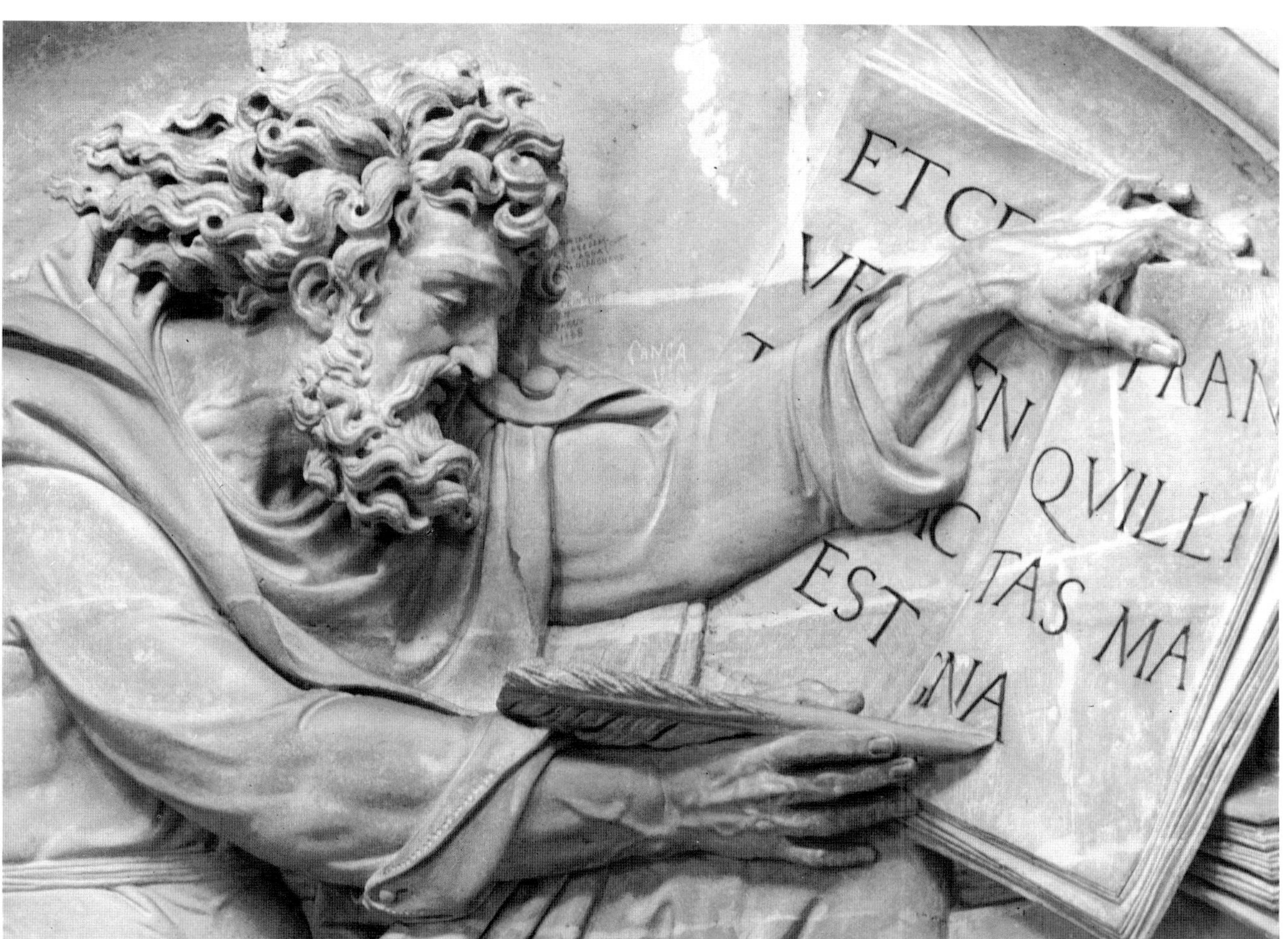

Plate 26
Detail of Plate 25.

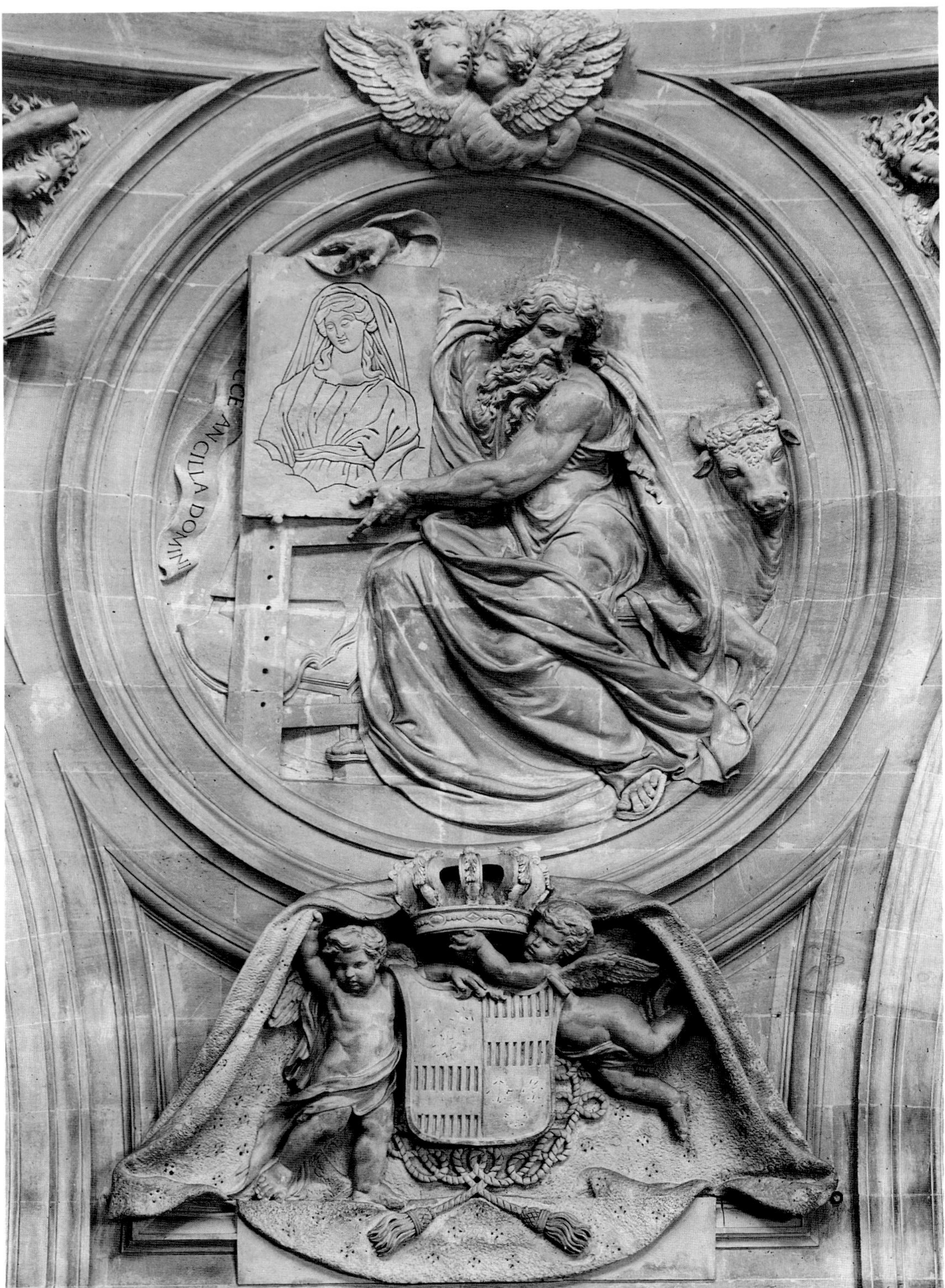

Plate 27
Michel Anguier, *Saint Luke*, stone relief, partly in the round, diameter 3.5 metres.
Paris, Val-de-Grâce.

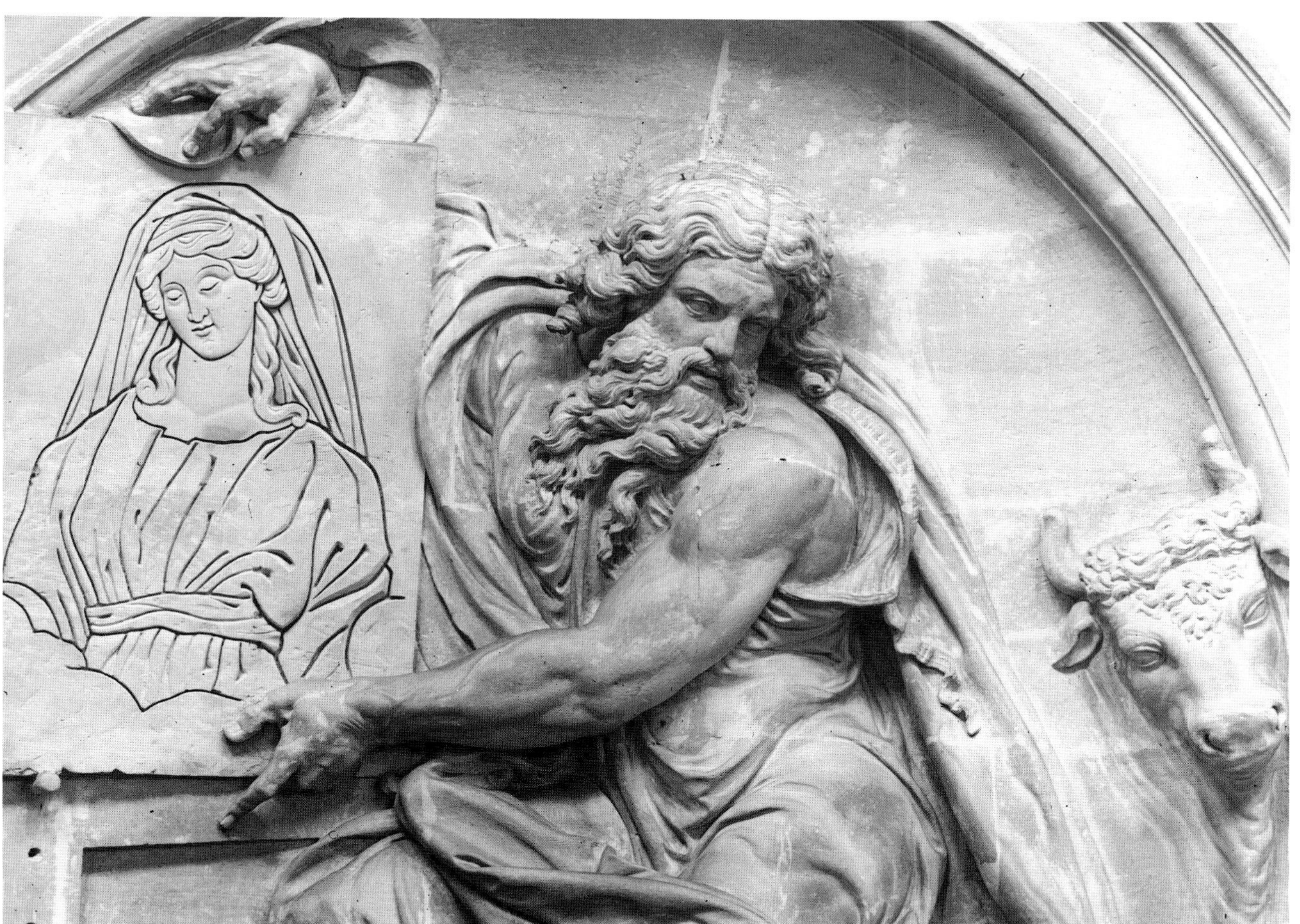

Plate 28
Detail of Plate 27.

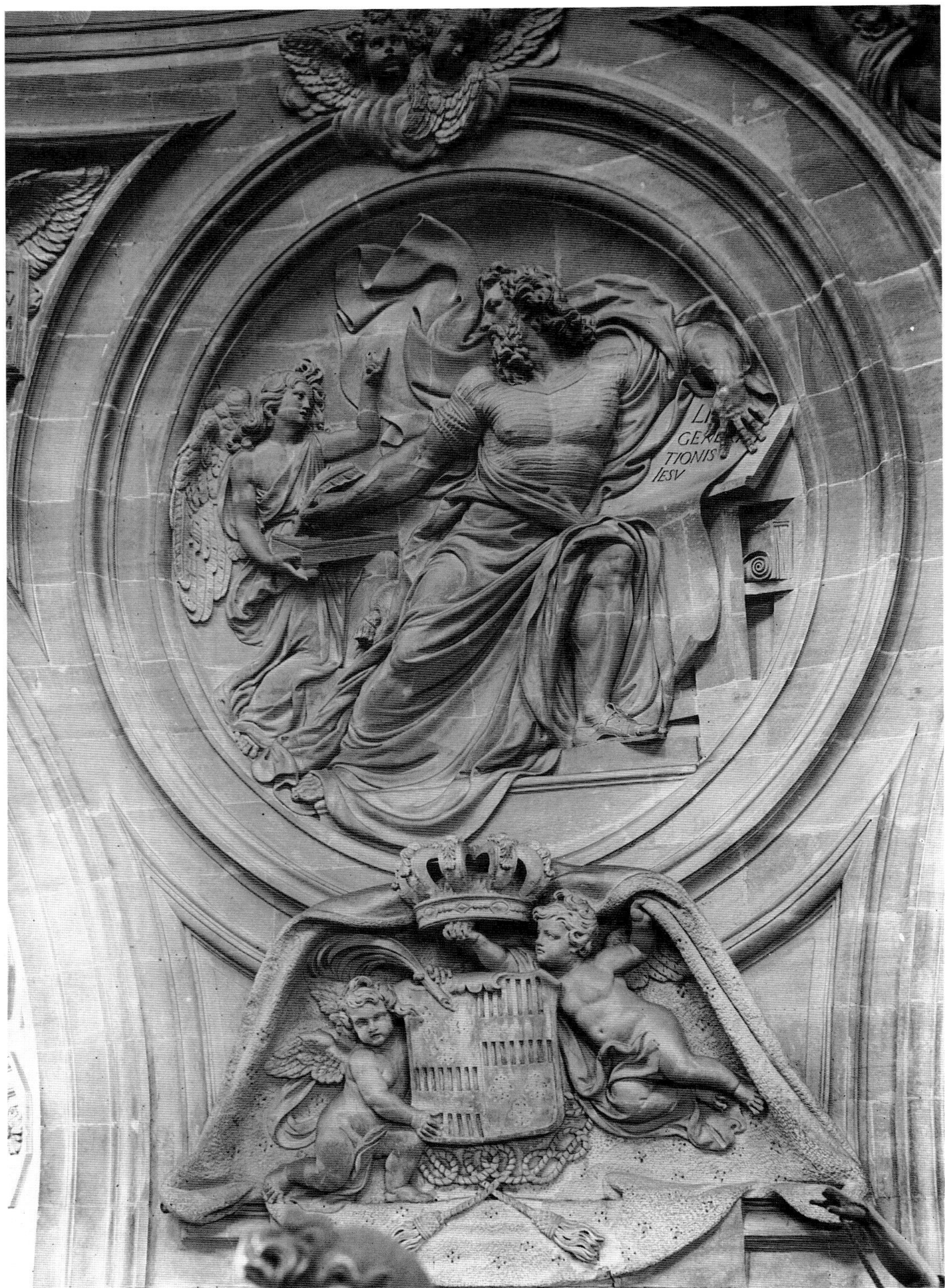

PLATE 29
Michel Anguier, *Saint Matthew*, stone relief, partly in the round, diameter 3.5 metres.
Paris, Val-de-Grâce.

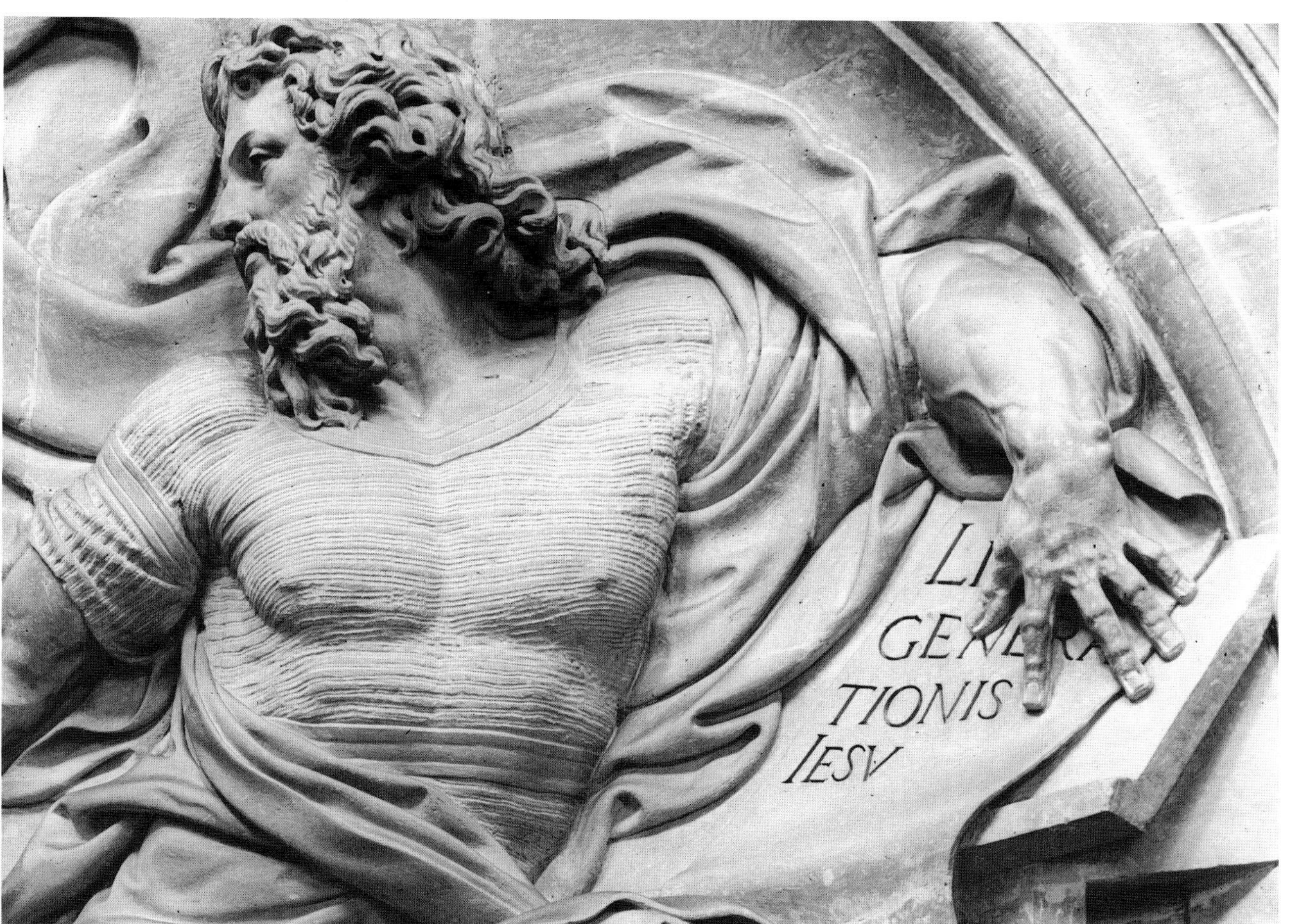

Plate 30
Detail of Plate 29.

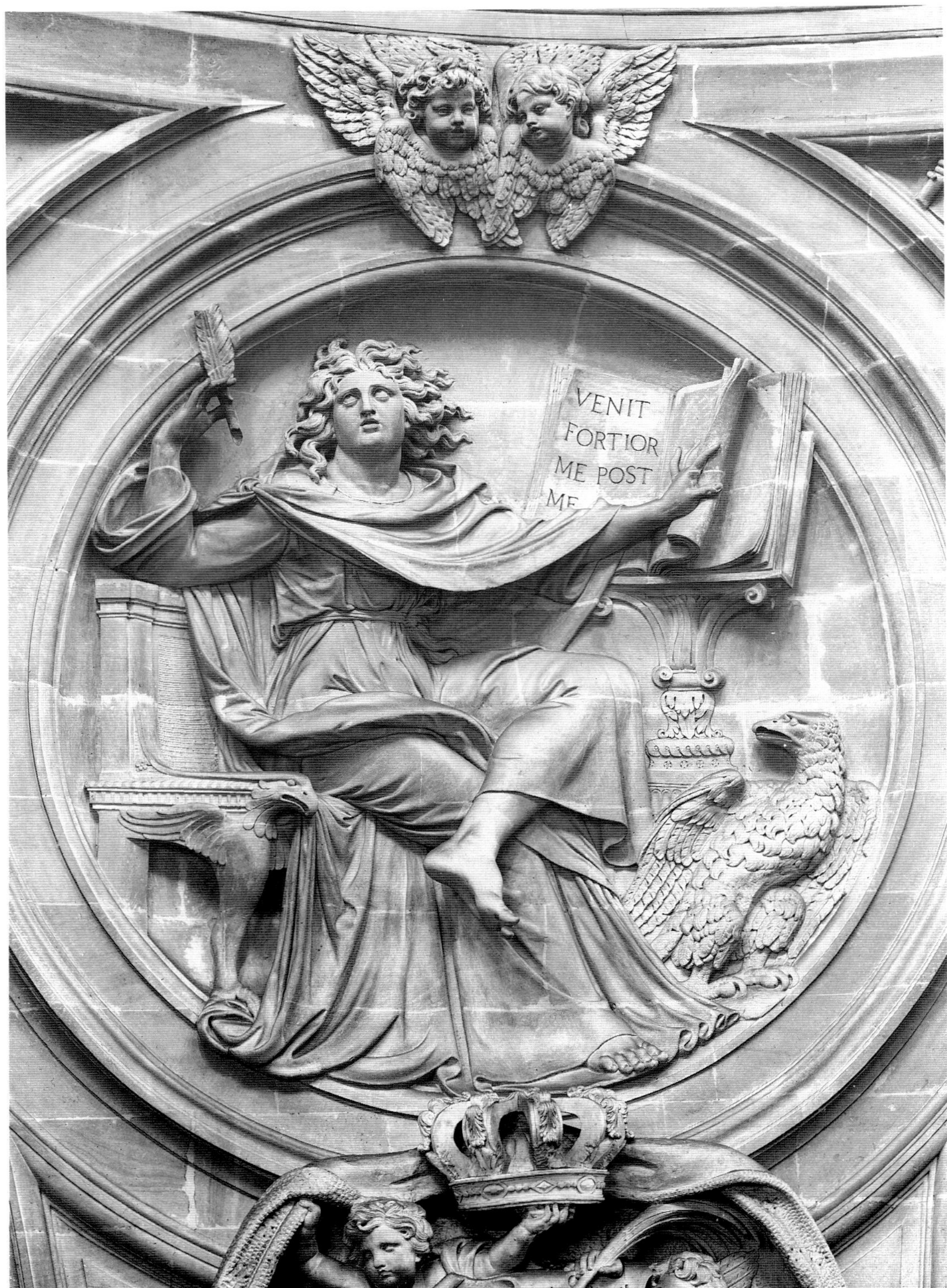

Plate 31
Michel Anguier, *Saint John*, stone relief, partly in the round, diameter 3.5 metres.
Paris, Val-de-Grâce.

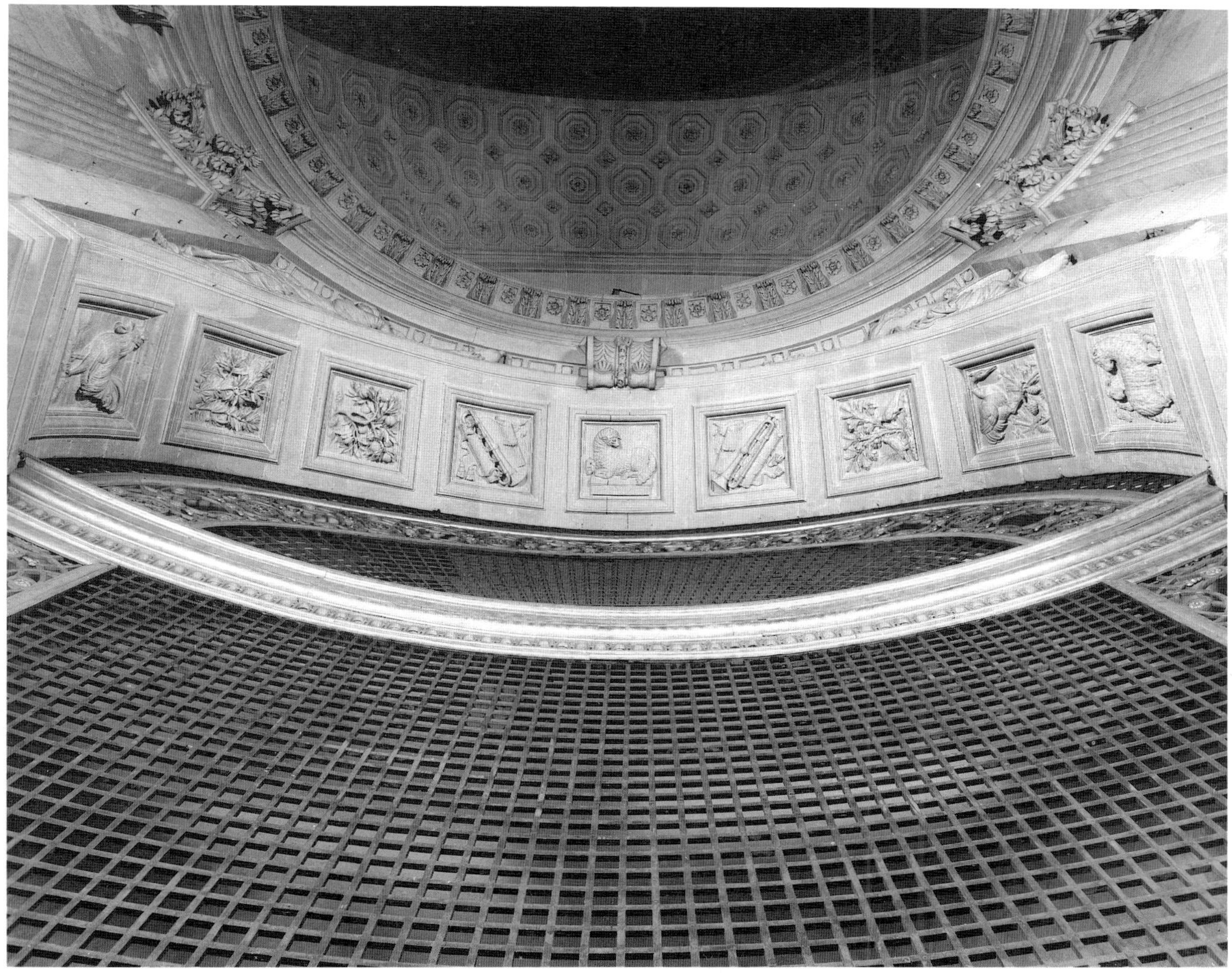

Plate 32
Michel Anguier, arch to the entrance of the Chapelle Saint-Louis, stone, executed between 1662 and 1667.
Paris, Val-de-Grâce.
The highest point – the *Agnus Dei* – is 6 metres from the floor.

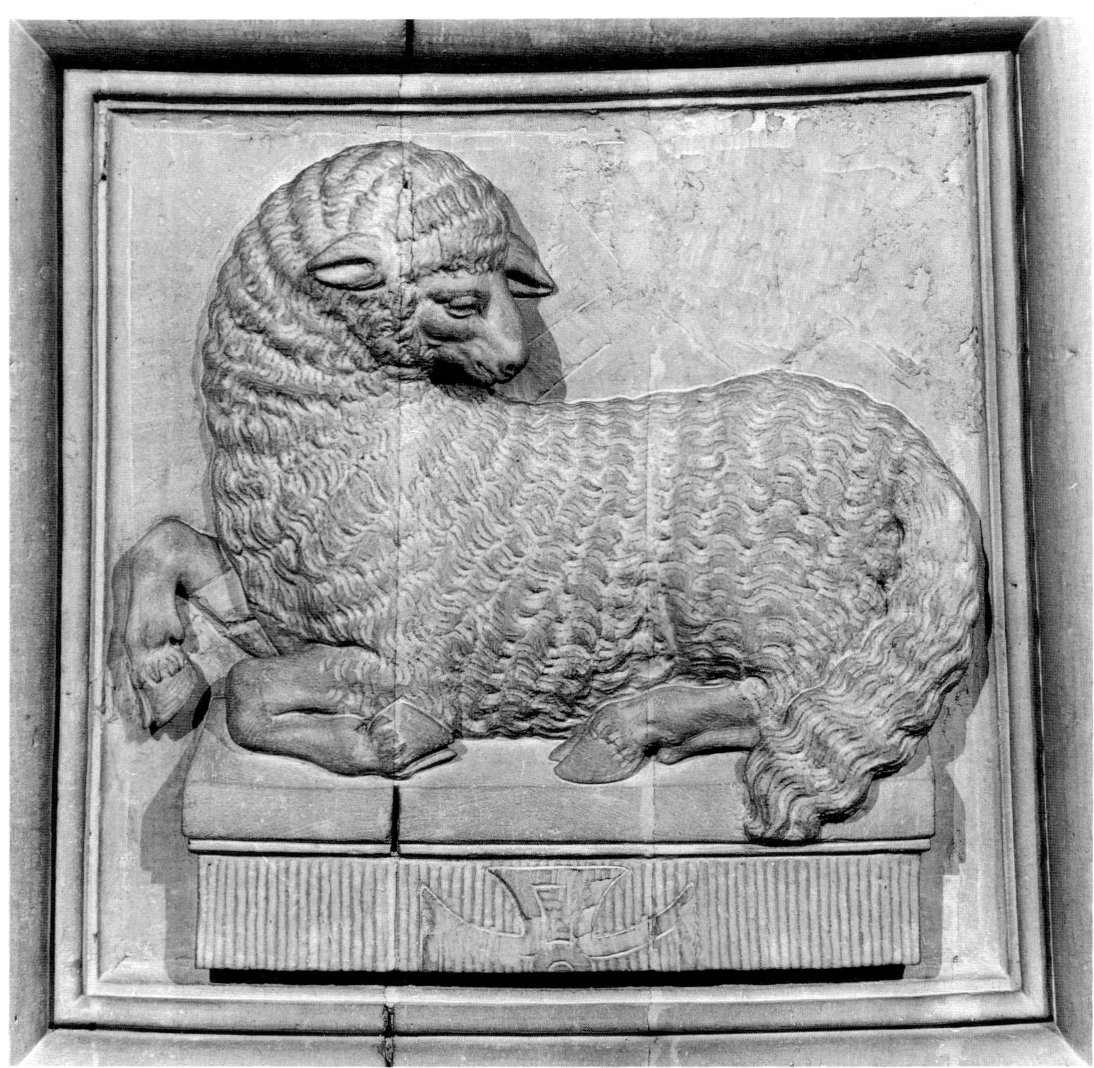

Plate 33
Detail of Plate 32: central panel depicting the *Agnus Dei*; the approximate length of the lamb is 65 cm.

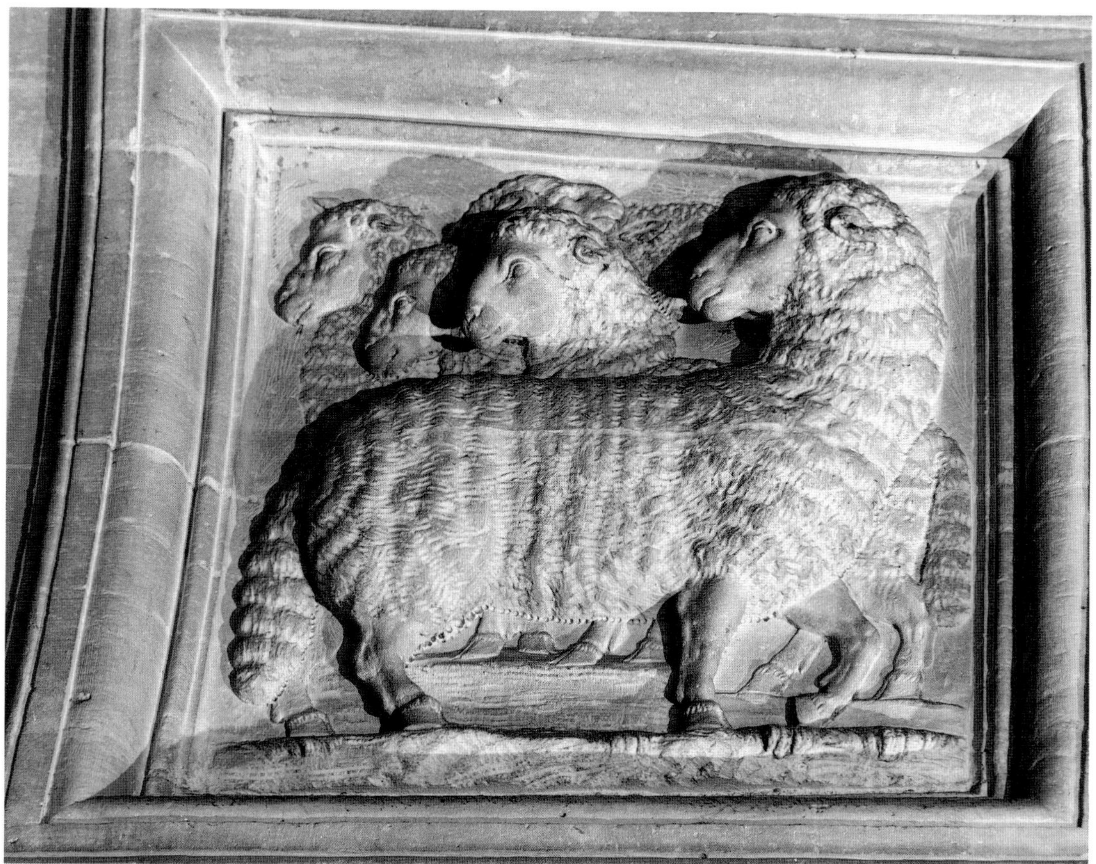

PLATE 34
Detail of PLATE 32: far right-hand panel of lambs; the scale is similar to PLATE 33.

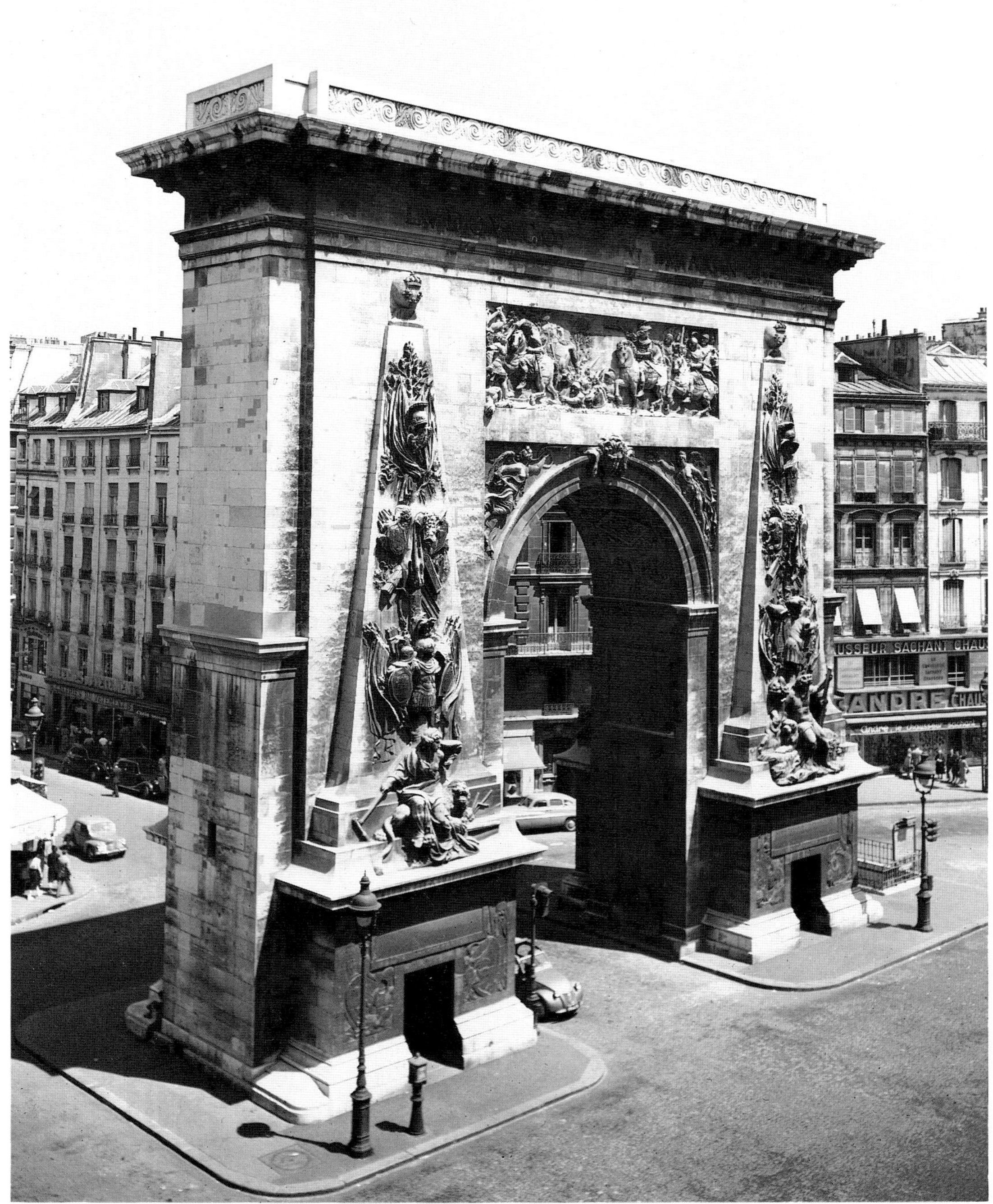

PLATE 35
François Blondel (architect) and Michel Anguier,
Porte Saint-Denis, Paris, 1674–1676.
Photograph circa 1945–1950.
Louis Gonse (1895) described the invention of this arch as 'the rarest and most perfect in (French) architecture'.

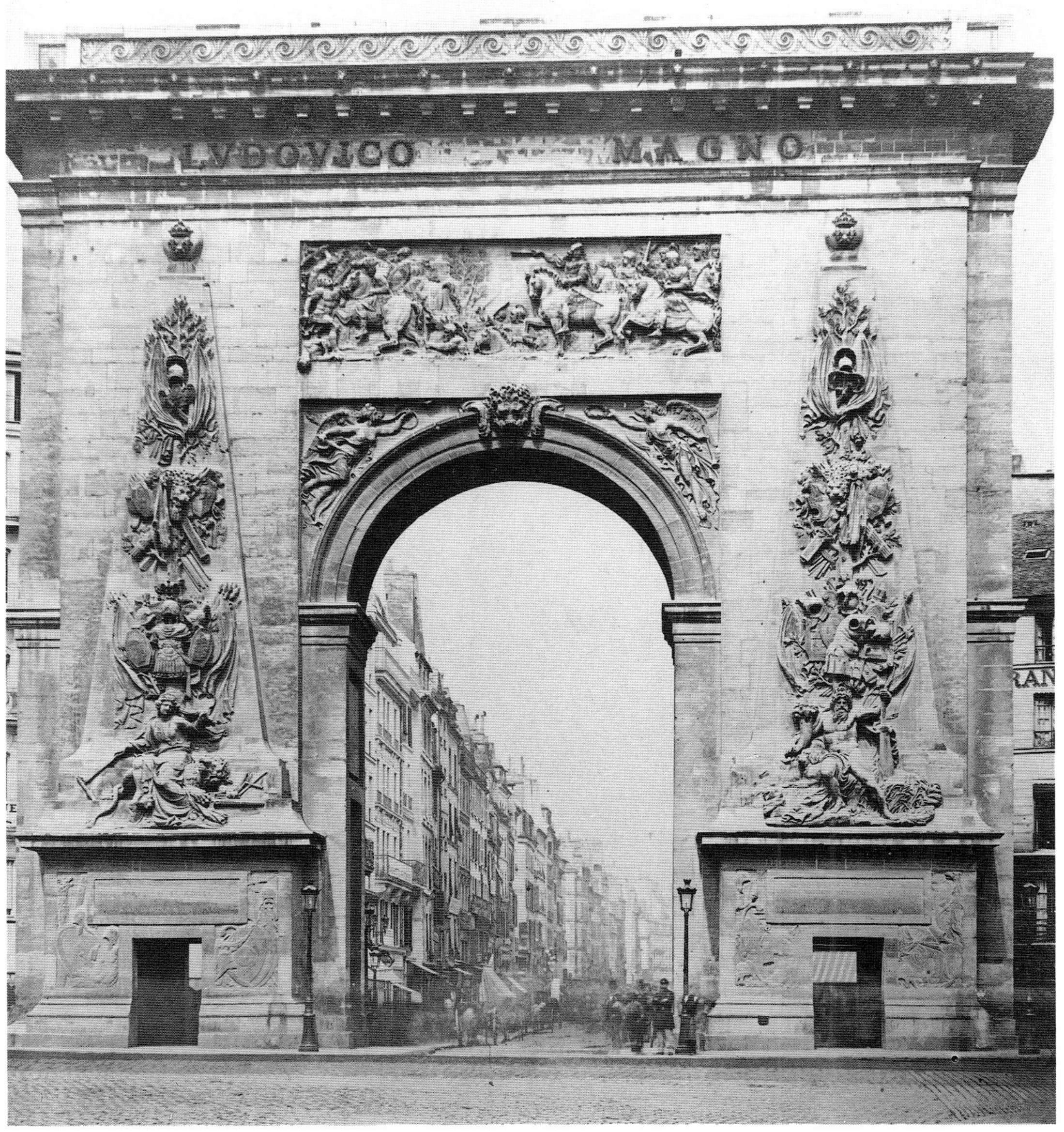

Plate 36
Frontal view of Plate 35. This photograph, taken circa 1910–1915, shows the sculptor's carvings before the deterioration of recent decades. The relief above is of *Louis XIV crossing the Rhine*; below are the allegories of *Holland* and *The Rhine*.

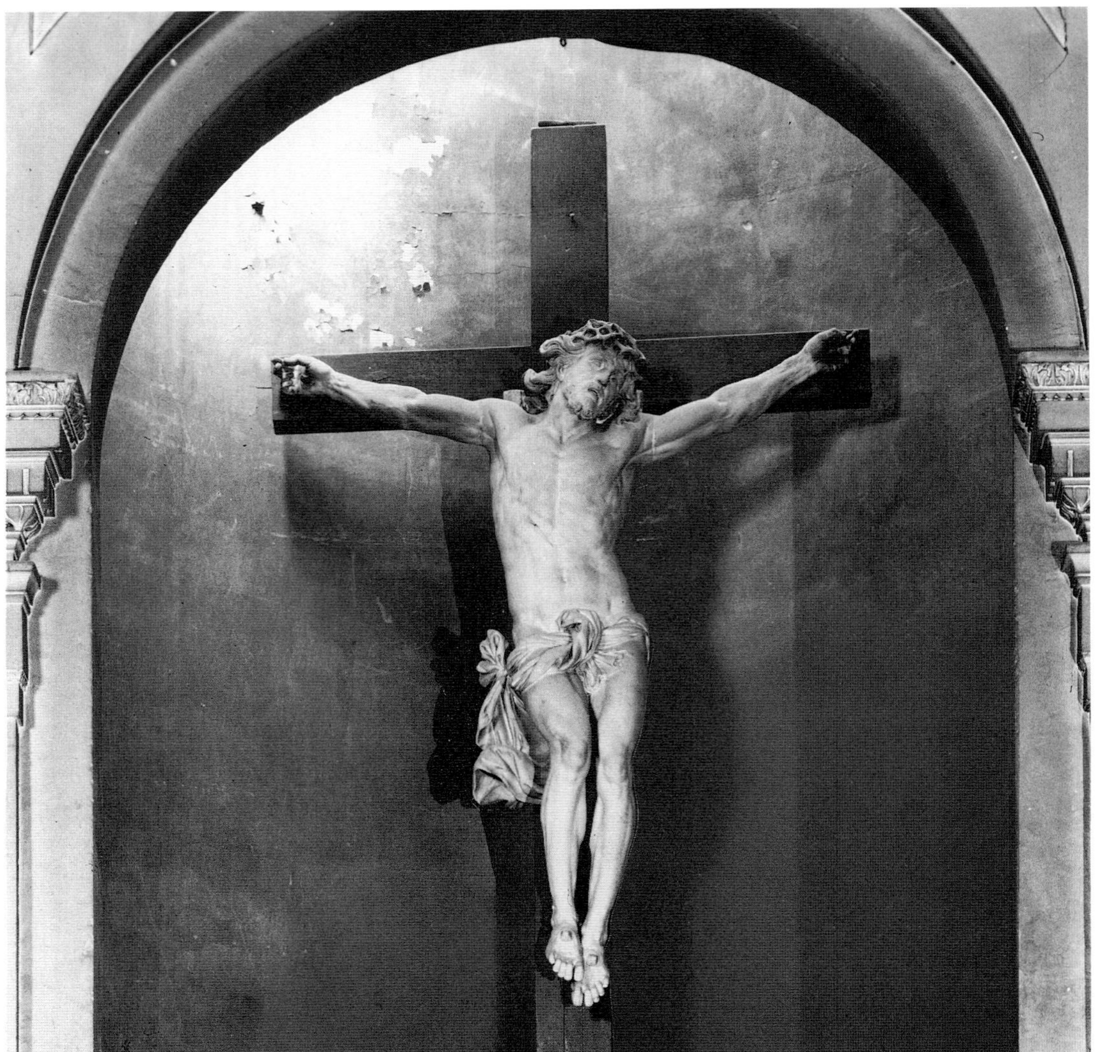

Plate 37A
Michel Anguier, *Christ crucified, alive*, marble, 1684,
height: 2.30 metres.
Paris, Eglise Saint-Roch, Chapelle du Calvaire.

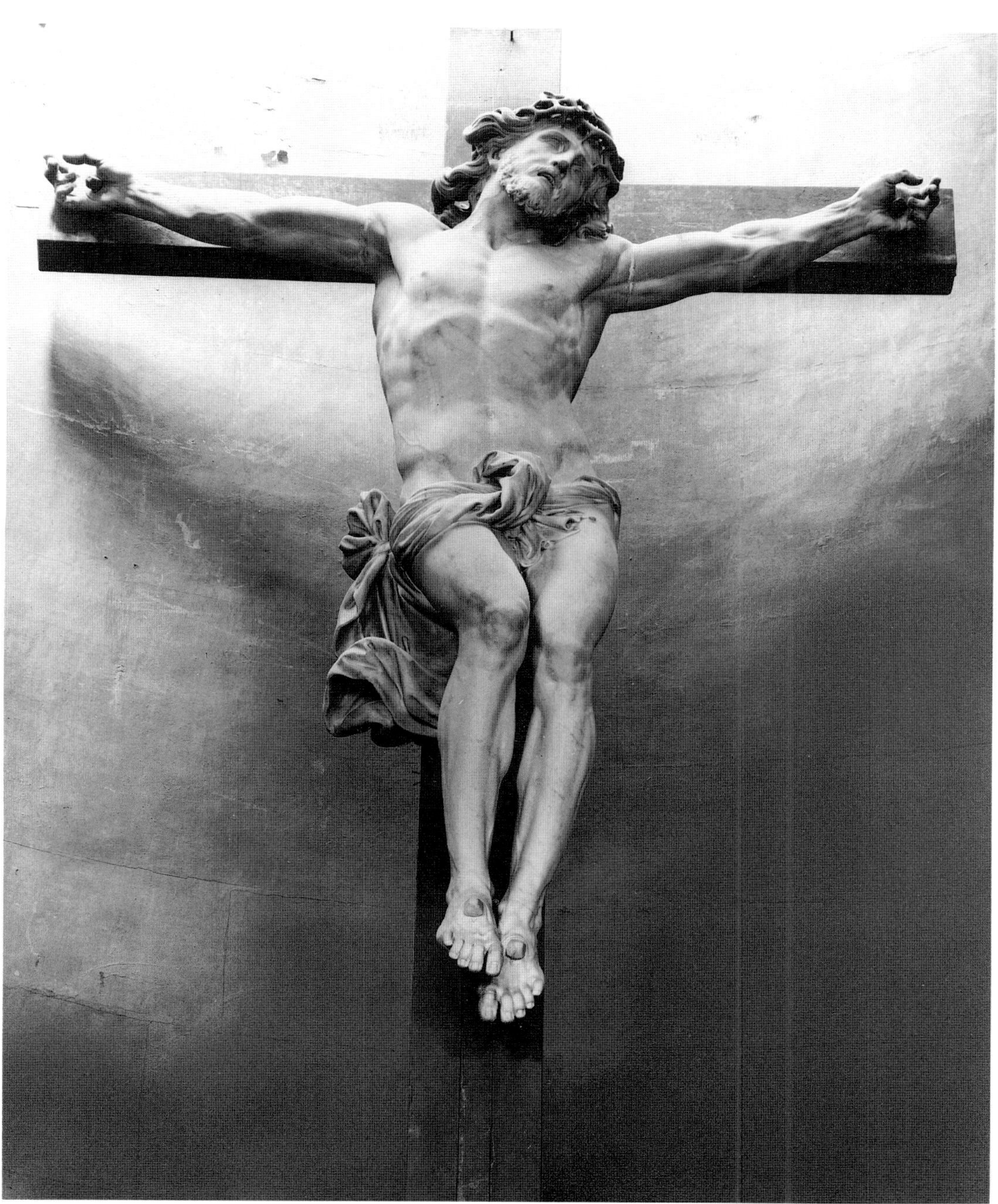

Plate 37b
A closer view, from below, of Plate 37a. This moving, little-known *Christ* was the sculptor's last major carving.

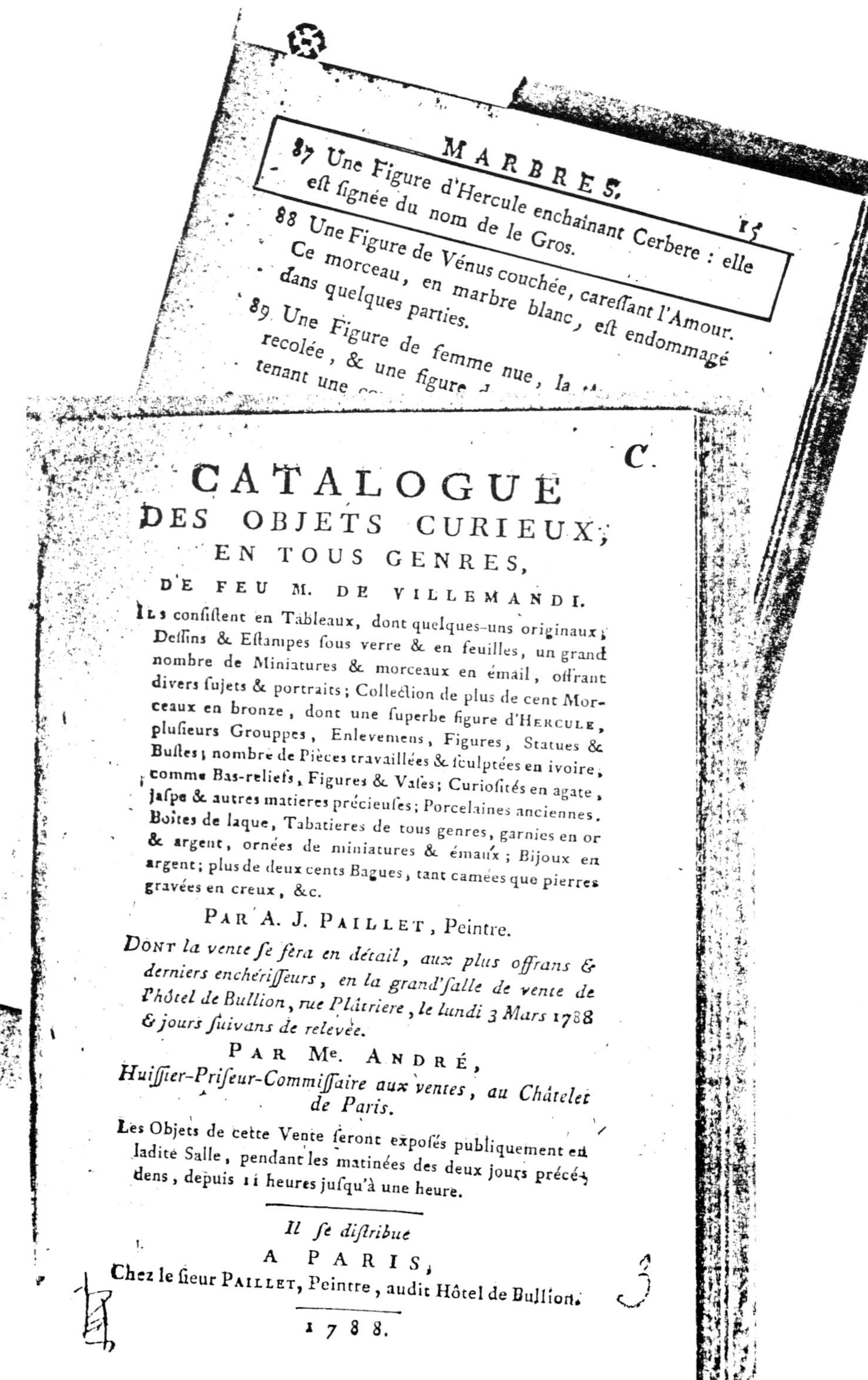

MARBRES. 15

87 Une Figure d'Hercule enchaînant Cerbere : elle eſt ſignée du nom de le Gros.

88 Une Figure de Vénus couchée, careſſant l'Amour. Ce morceau, en marbre blanc, eſt endommagé dans quelques parties.

89 Une Figure de femme nue, la ... recolée, & une figure ... tenant une ...

C.

CATALOGUE
DES OBJETS CURIEUX,
EN TOUS GENRES,
DE FEU M. DE VILLEMANDI.

ILS conſiſtent en Tableaux, dont quelques-uns originaux; Deſſins & Eſtampes ſous verre & en feuilles, un grand nombre de Miniatures & morceaux en émail, offrant divers ſujets & portraits; Collection de plus de cent Morceaux en bronze, dont une ſuperbe figure d'HERCULE, pluſieurs Grouppes, Enlevemens, Figures, Statues & Buſtes; nombre de Pièces travaillées & ſculptées en ivoire, comme Bas-reliefs, Figures & Vaſes; Curioſités en agate, jaſpe & autres matieres précieuſes; Porcelaines anciennes, Boites de laque, Tabatieres de tous genres, garnies en or & argent, ornées de miniatures & émaux; Bijoux en argent; plus de deux cents Bagues, tant camées que pierres gravées en creux, &c.

PAR A. J. PAILLET, Peintre.

DONT la vente ſe fera en détail, aux plus offrans & derniers enchériſſeurs, en la grand'ſalle de vente de l'hôtel de Bullion, rue Plâtriere, le lundi 3 Mars 1788 & jours ſuivans de relevée.

PAR Me. ANDRÉ,
Huiſſier-Priſeur-Commiſſaire aux ventes, au Châtelet de Paris.

Les Objets de cette Vente ſeront expoſés publiquement en ladite Salle, pendant les matinées des deux jours précédens, depuis 11 heures juſqu'à une heure.

Il ſe diſtribue
A PARIS,
Chez le ſieur PAILLET, Peintre, audit Hôtel de Bullion.

1788.

PLATE 38
Paris, Villemandi sale, 1788. Title page of catalogue and entry for lot 87.

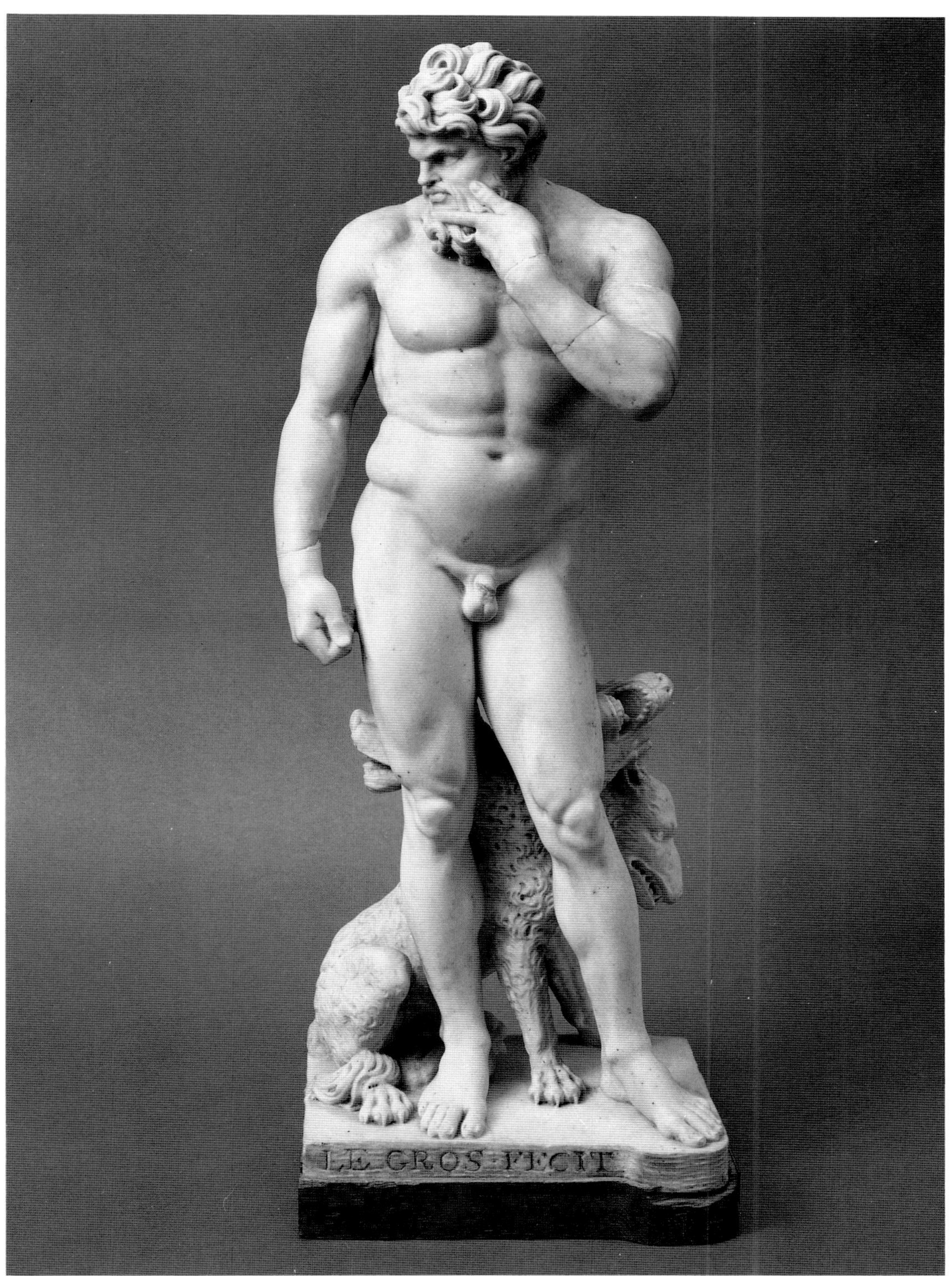

PLATE 39
Michel Anguier, *Pluto*, marble. Before conservation.

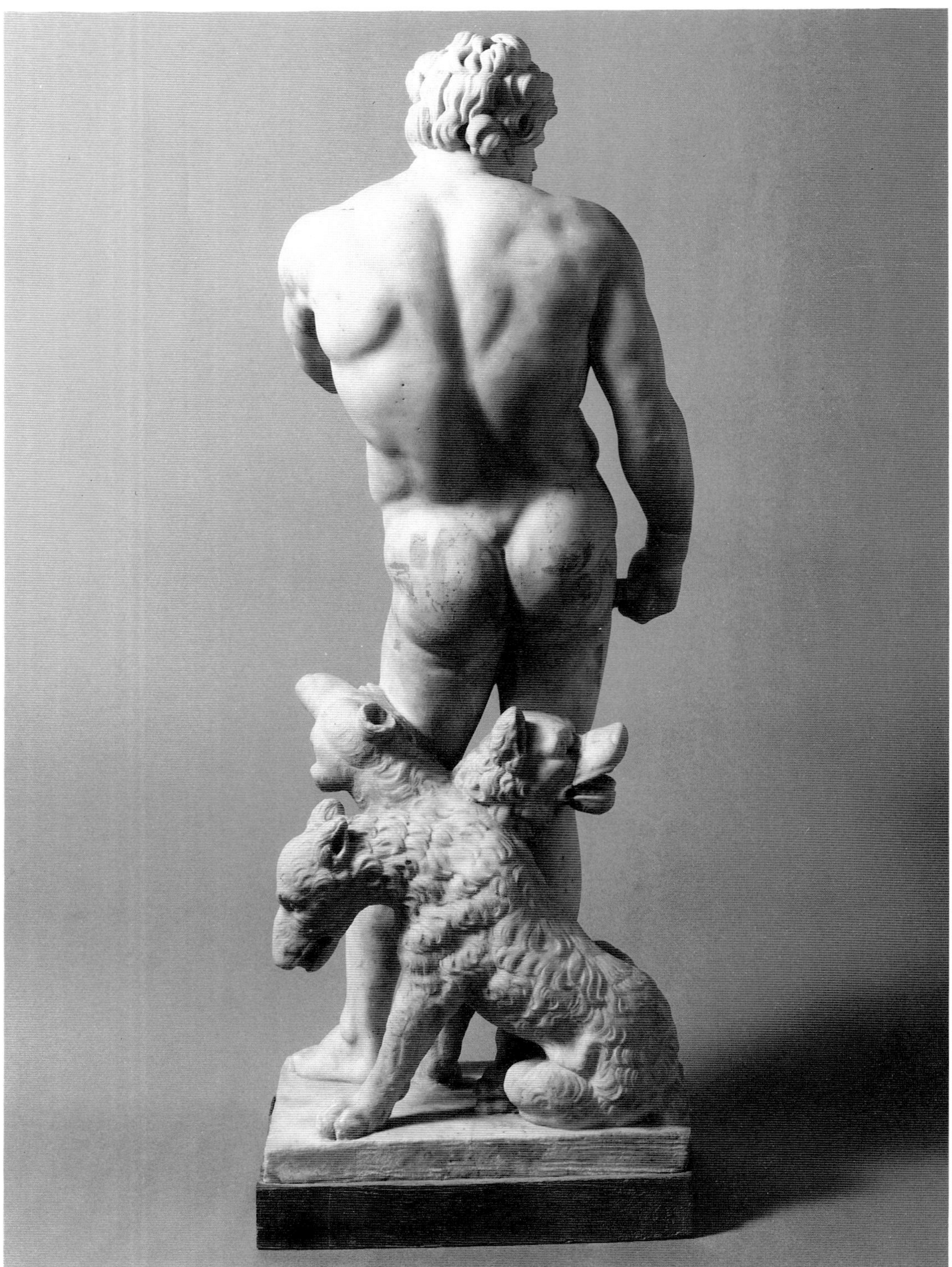

PLATE 40
Rear view of PLATE 39. Notice the treatment of the fur and the ears of Cerberus.

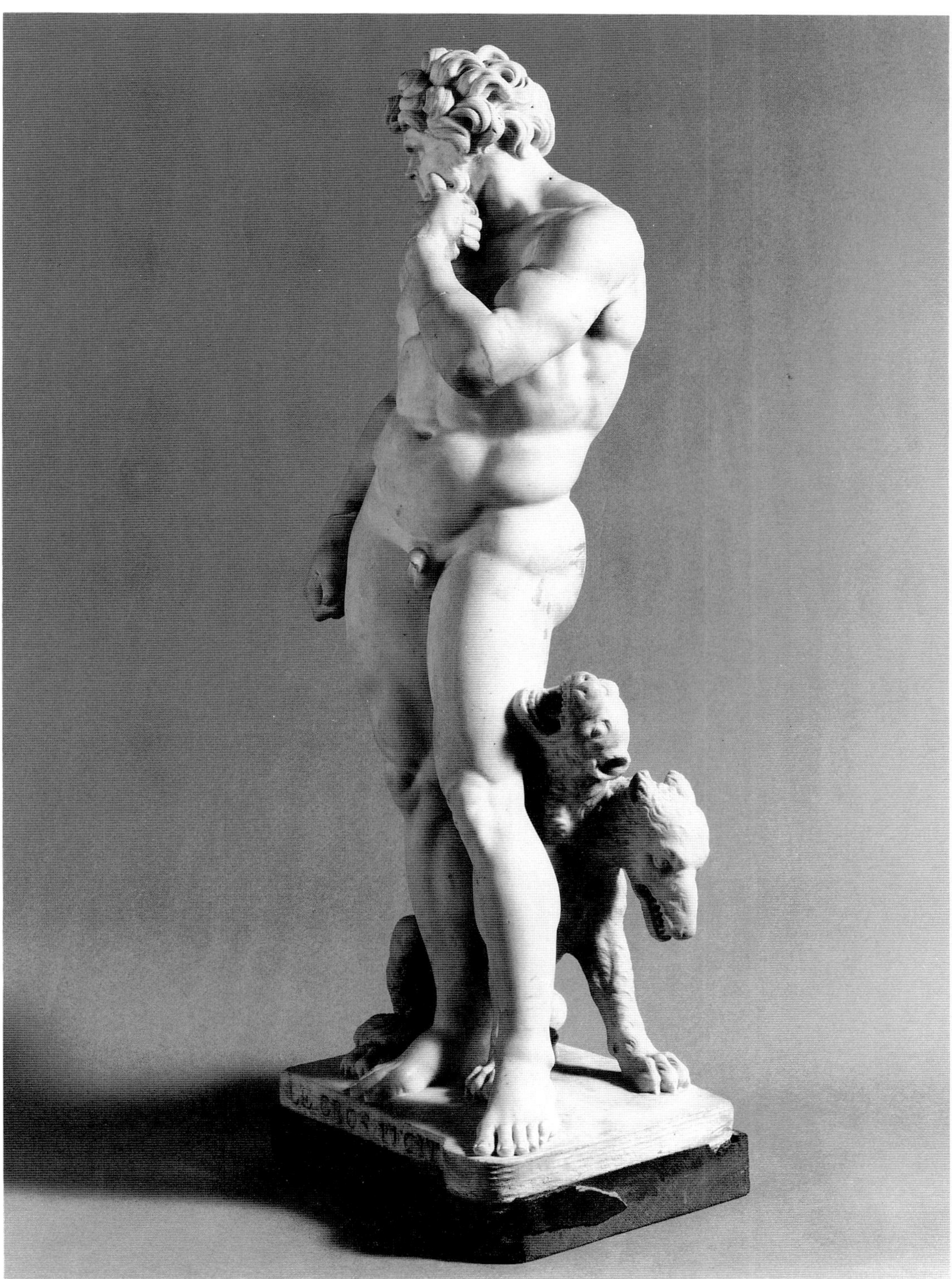

PLATE 41
Side view of PLATE 39. The shallow, unfinished wood base was gouged within to fit the convex underside, enabling the figure to stand.

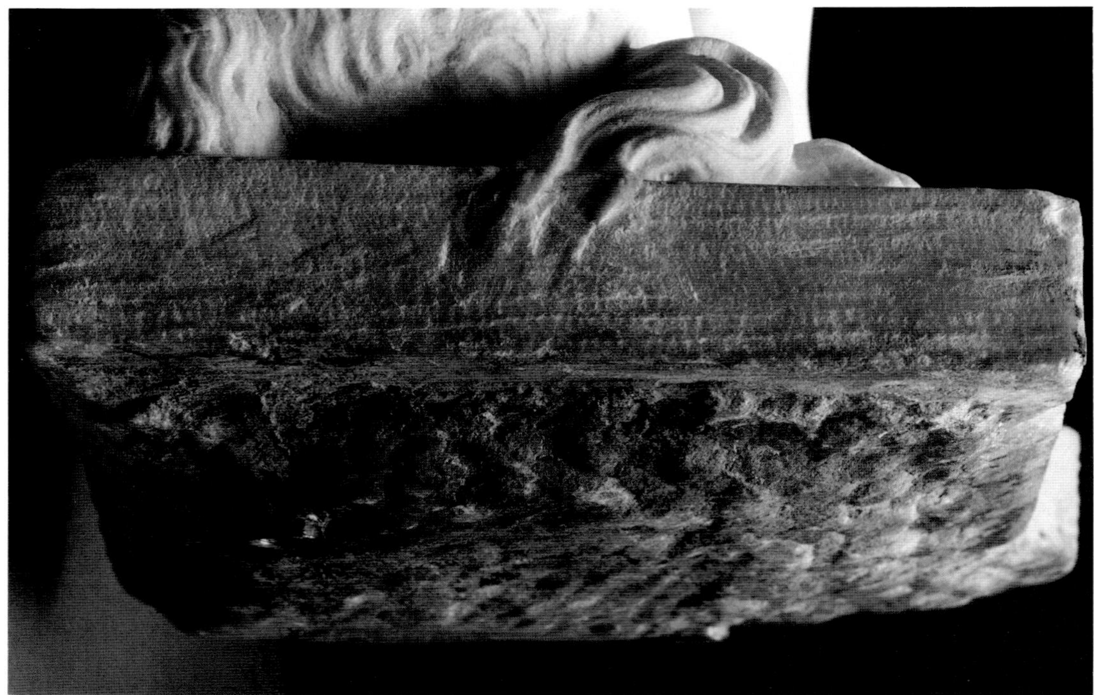

Plate 42
Detail of Plate 1: the convex underside of the sculpture.

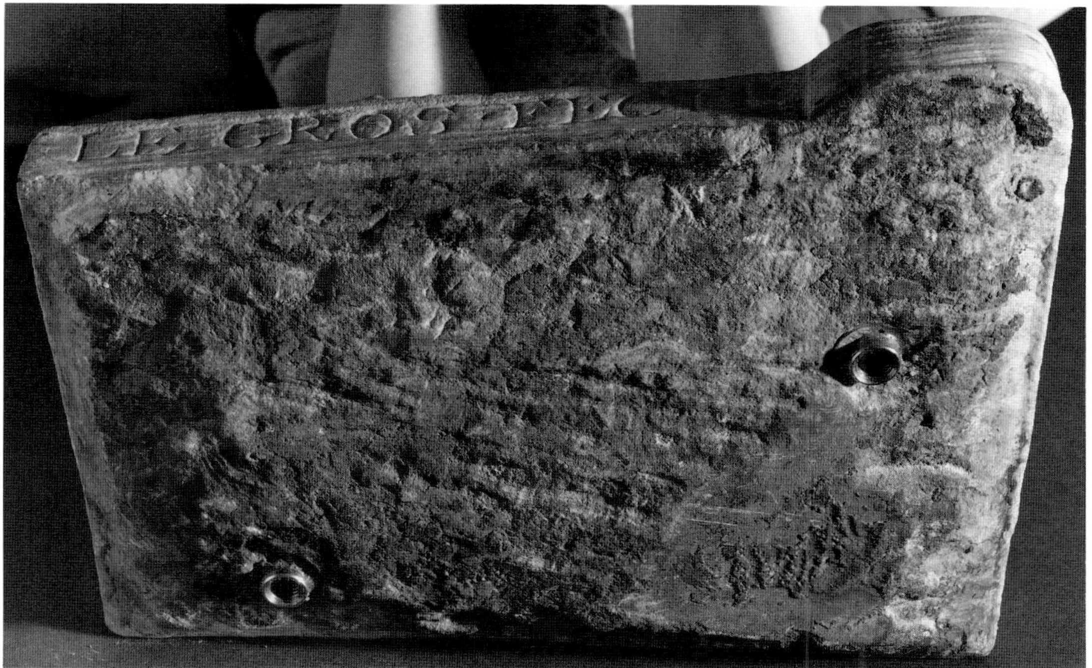

PLATE 43
Detail of PLATE 1: the underside of the sculpture, showing the remaining, original flat area.

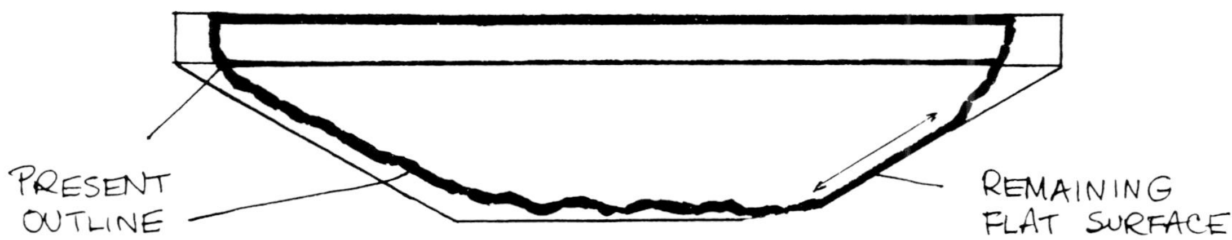

PLATE 44
Sketch showing suggested original form of the underside of the sculpture, as conceived by Anne Brodrick.

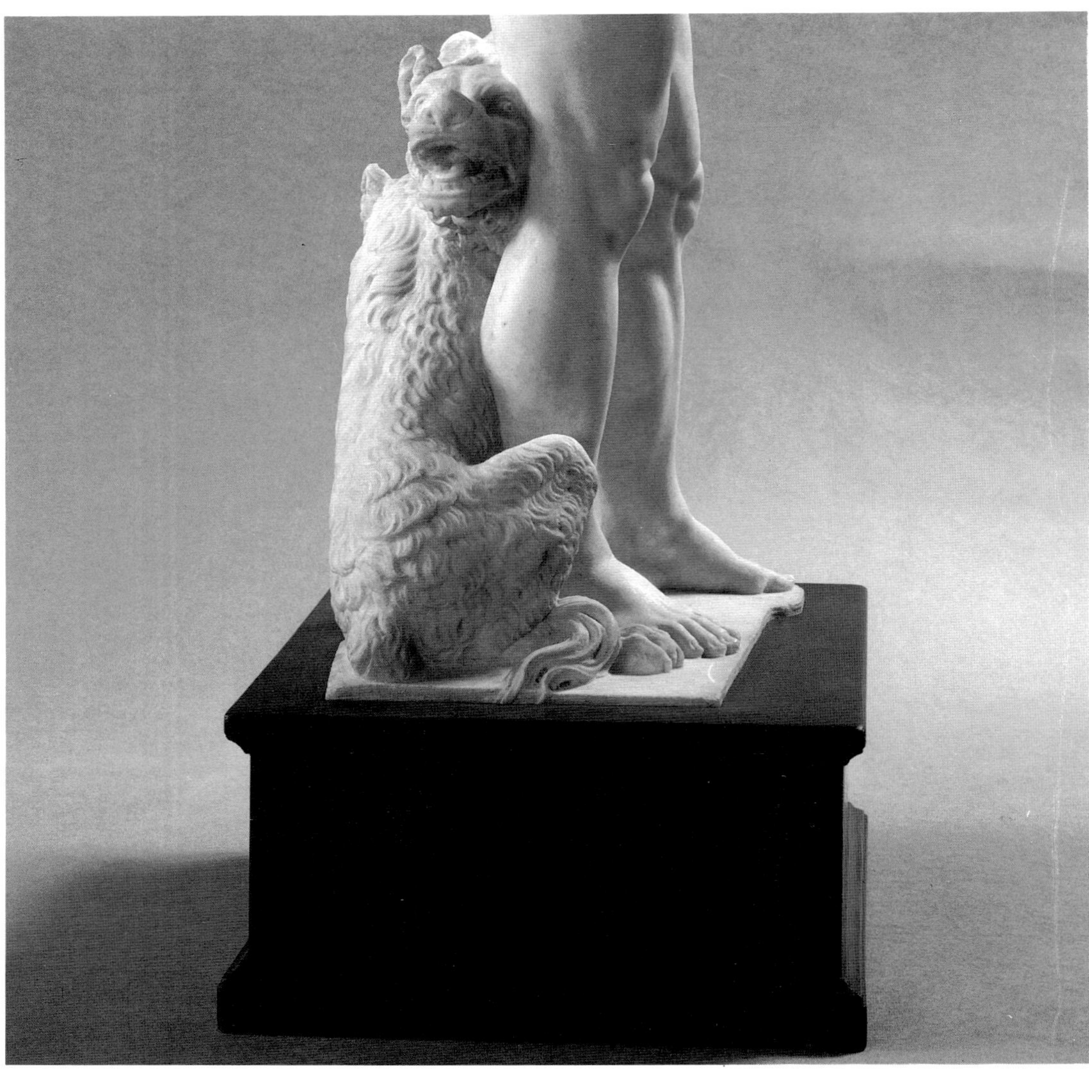

PLATE 45
Detail of PLATE 1: the marble sculpture is now set in a slate-coloured wood base, concealing the later inscription.

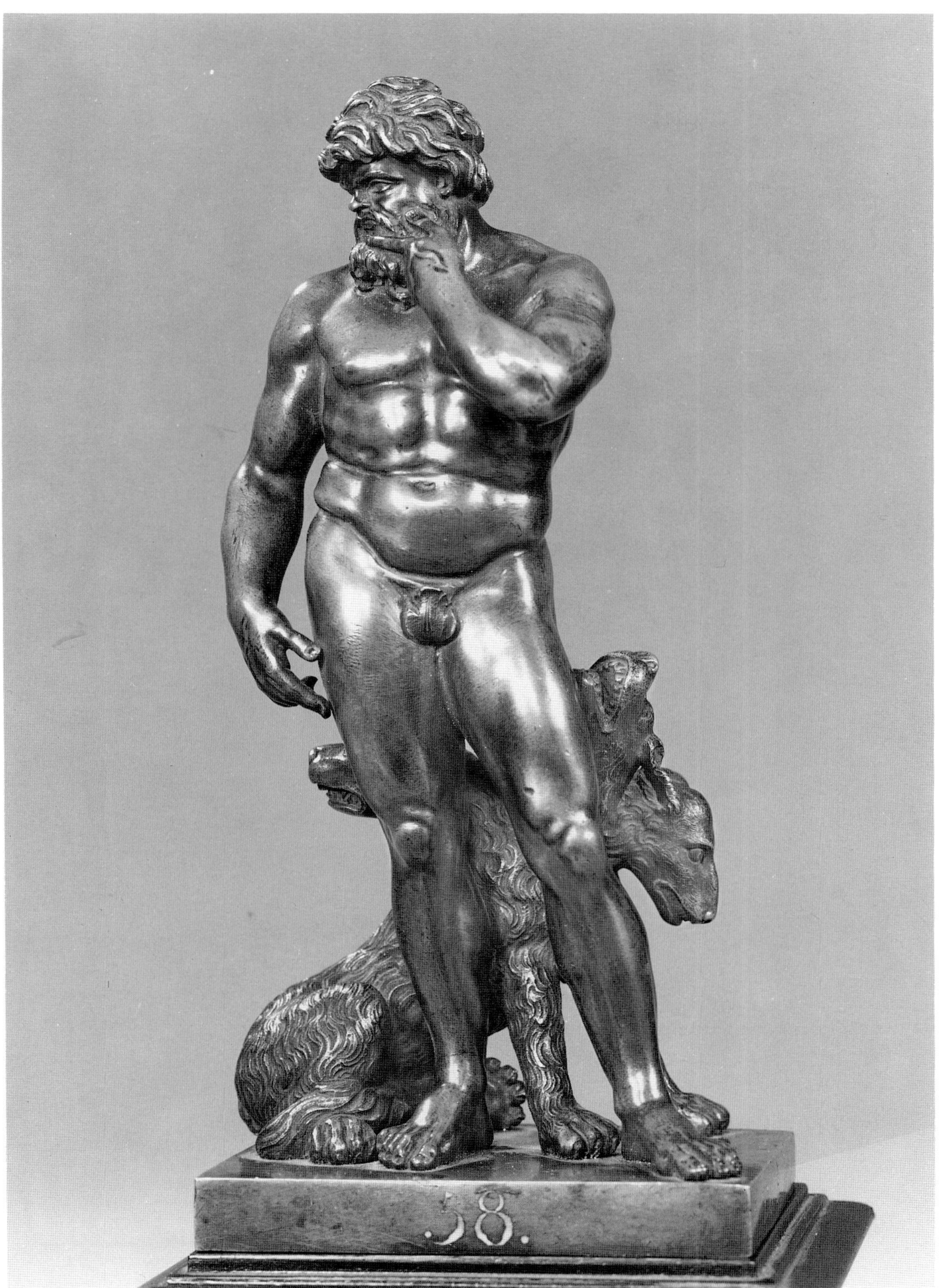

PLATE 46
Pluto, after Michel Anguier, bronze, late seventeenth century, height: 24.5 cm. Purchased for Augustus the Strong in 1699. Dresden, Grünes Gewölbe.

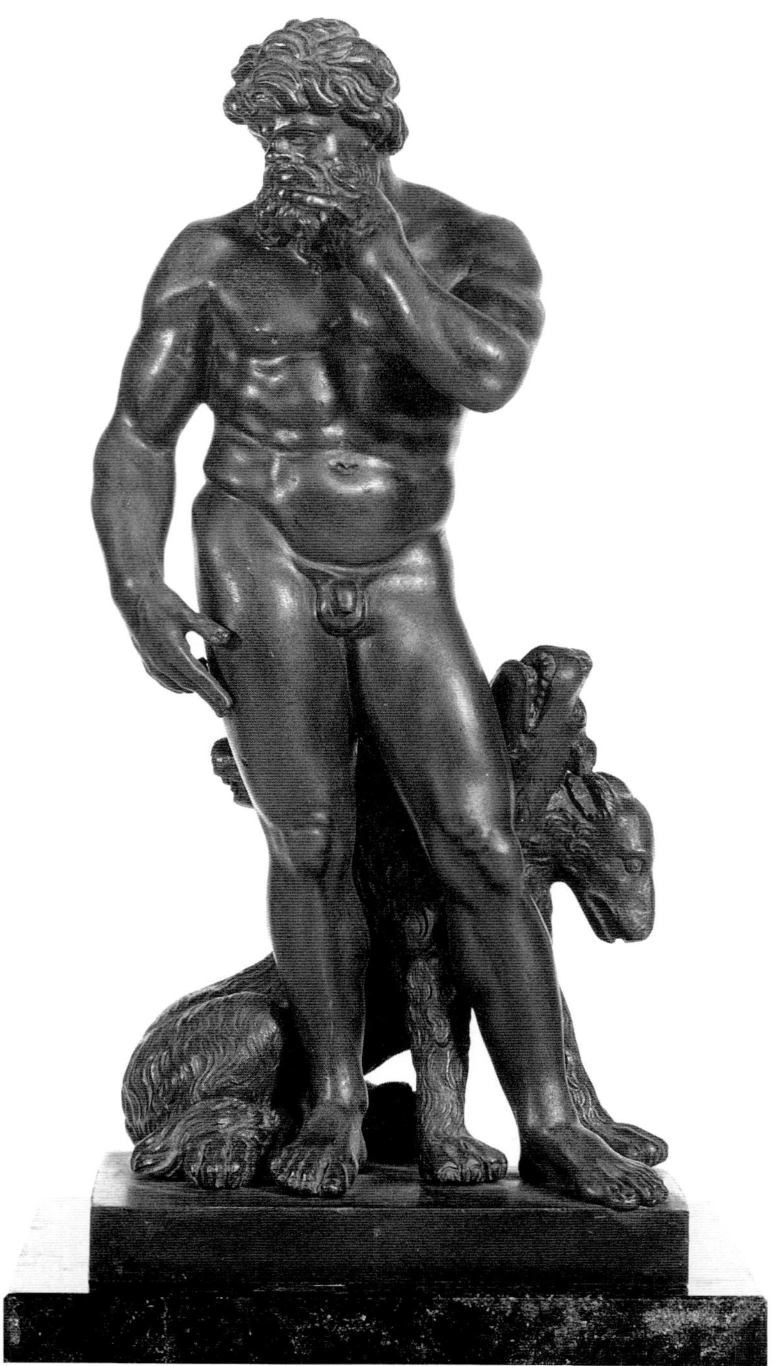

PLATE 47
Pluto, after Michel Anguier, bronze, before 1767, height: 23.5 cm.
Kassel, Staatliche Kunstsammlungen.
The only known bronze depicting the god naked.

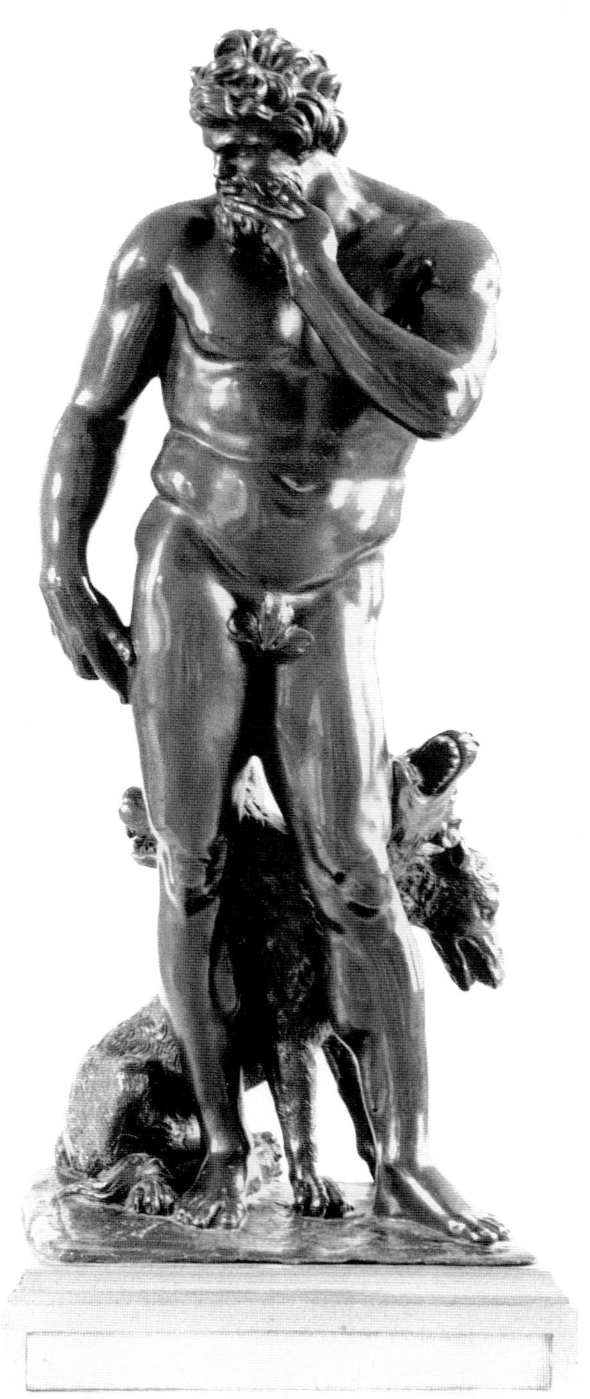

PLATE 48
Pluto, after Michel Anguier, bronze, eighteenth century, height: 54 cm
Paris, Musée Carnavalet, Collection of Henriette Bouvier.

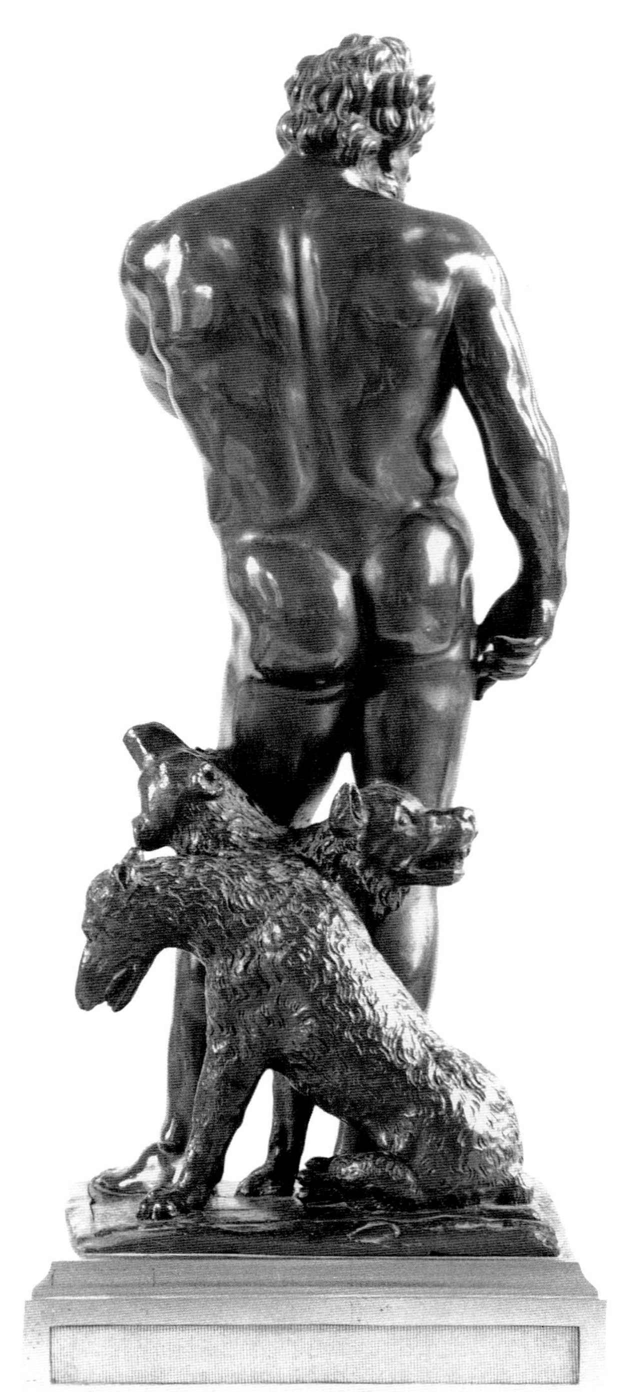

PLATE 49
Rear view of PLATE 48.

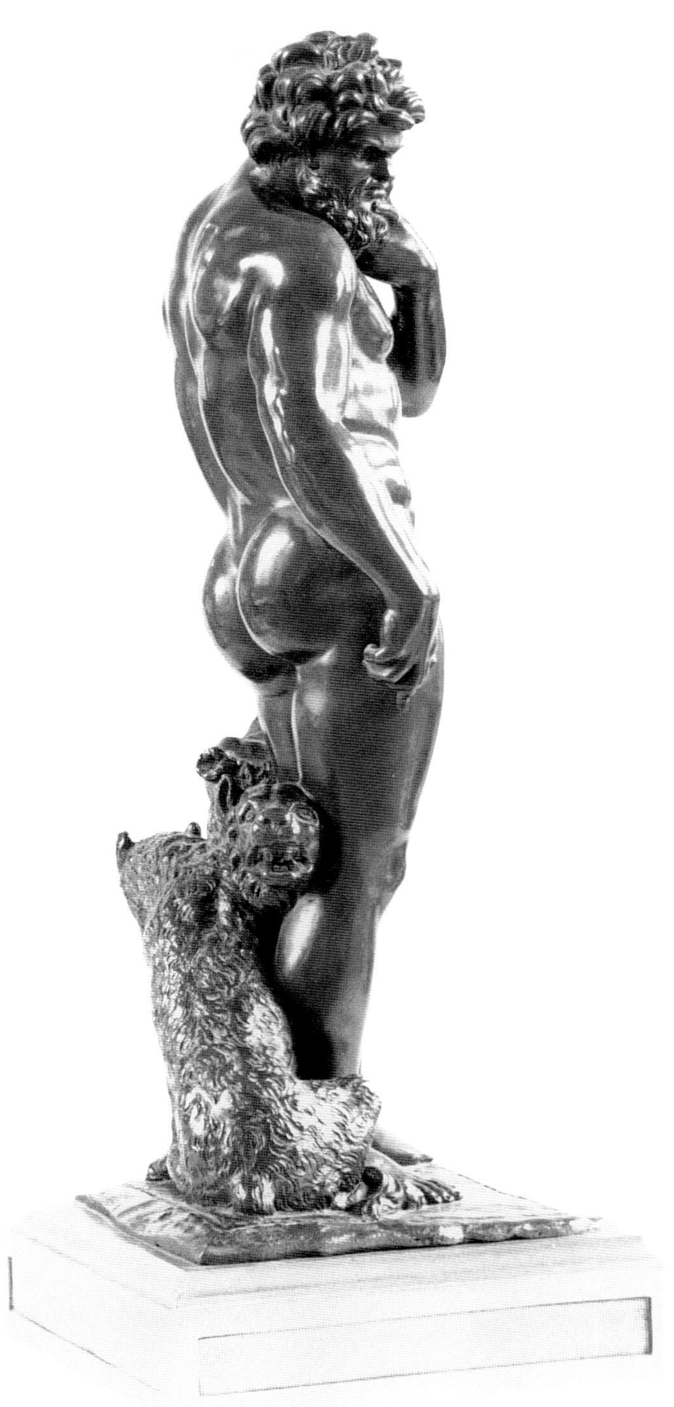

PLATE 50
Side view of PLATE 48. Notice the flattened back of Cerberus and compare with PLATE 2.

Photograph Acknowledgements

Frontispiece (colour) and detail (colour):
Michael Fear, London.

Portrait:
Herzog August Bibliothek, Wolfenbüttel.

Plates 1–6, 23, 42, 43, 45:
John Hammond, London.

Plate 7:
Trustees of the British Museum, London.

Plates 8–18:
Bibliothèque Nationale, Paris.

Plate 19:
Cliché Réunion des Musées Nationaux, Paris.

Plates 20–22:
The Conway Library, Courtauld Institute, London.

Plate 24:
Edimedia, Paris. Photo: *Connaissance des Arts.*

Plates 25–31; 35–37b:
Arch. Photo., Paris, © Spadem

Plates 32–34:
B. Acloque/CNMHS, © Spadem

Plates 39–41:
Michael Fear, London.

Plate 46:
Staatliche Kunstsammlungen, Dresden.

Plate 47:
Staatliche Kunstsammlungen, Kassel.

Plates 48–50:
Photothèque des Musées de la Ville de Paris by Spadem, 1990.

Index

Plate numbers are in **bold**
Superior figures refer to notes